Dr. Robert Smith Jr. is one of the most compelling voices in American preaching today. Drawing on the wisdom of the African-American tradition with its anchor in the words and actions of Holy Scripture, *Doctrine That Dances* describes the preacher's task in a way that is at once personal, passionate, and provocative. This book describes the kind of preaching that is at the heart of the awakening that must come.

Timothy George
Founding dean of Beeson Divinity School
and a senior editor of *Christianity Today*

One of the great needs of our day is for creative, substantive, and biblically faithful doctrinal preaching. Robert Smith's new work, *Doctrine That Dances*, insightfully and helpfully addresses this need. A masterful preacher and teacher himself, Smith provides direction for students, young pastors, and veteran preachers alike. Pulpits across the land will be strengthened as preachers implement the guidance offered in this volume. *Doctrine That Dances* will become mandatory reading for a new generation of preachers. It is a joy to recommend this marvelous work.

David Dockery
President, Union University, Jackson, Tennessee

May I commend to you Dr. Smith's new book, *Doctrine That Dances*. It is truly a book that is desperately needed among pastors, teachers, and professors today. To use Dr. Smith's own words, "Worshippers are being served sermonic snacks instead of the doctrinal depth of the Word of God." A truer word hath never been spoken. This book combines the depth of scholarly research with practical and useful advice for the preacher and listener. A book such as this will go a long way in combating the spiritual shallowness that besets the modern-day church. You'll be blessed and challenged by the reading of this new book.

Dr. Frank S. Page
President of the Southern Baptist Convention

Robert Smith preaches with a zeal for God's Word that is engaging, enlightening, and inspiring. In *Doctrine That Dances*, he details the principles that delight and empower him in order to share with us his understanding of gospel joy that makes the soul sing and the heart dance.

Dr. Bryan Chapell,
President, Covenant Seminary, St. Louis, Missouri

Dr. Robert Smith Jr. has given to all of us an invaluable manual for doctrinal preaching—the summit of the sermonic undertaking. Almost every page sparkles with mind- arresting, heart-touching metaphors that dance and sing, many bearing winsome traces of the author's ethnic legacy. This is a classic enchiridion. Preachers, lovers of preaching, get it!

Gardner Taylor, D.D.
Pastor Emeritus, The Concord Baptist Church of Christ

Dr. Robert Smith has become one of our favorite convention preachers. Now, his unique style and remarkable gift of preaching have graced this timely book. The greatest need of the pulpit in our time is sound doctrinal preaching. In this outstanding book, Dr. Smith challenges the proclaimer to discover the anchor for his preaching in the doctrine of God's Word. This book should be required reading for every seminary student and every seasoned preacher of the gospel.

J. Robert White
Executive Director, Georgia Baptist Convention

Wow, what a book! Reading the introduction whets your appetite for the entire volume. It will transform dull, passionless rhetoric into joyful, dynamic, and creative preaching by the power of the Holy Spirit. Sound theology produces great hymnology, resulting in glorious doxology. *Doctrine That Dancing* unites this trilogy and makes me say, "May I have the next dance?" Read it, you must!

Cliff Barrows
Program Director, Billy Graham Evangelistic Association

Dr. Robert Smith's book is both theological and biographical. Each chapter is choreographed to assist the preacher, teacher, and interested reader to get in step with the movements of doctrinal preaching. This book will become a homiletical coach to anyone interested in developing biblical theological sermons. Every serious student of the Scripture should read this masterpiece and dance the steps of doctrinal preaching.

Dr. Ralph Douglas West
The Church Without Walls, Houston, Texas

In *Doctrine That Dances*, Dr. Smith has produced—through scholarship, experience, and inspiration—a work that moves effortlessly between mind and the spirit. Far from offering a template for the simple imitation of great preaching, Dr. Smith leads us in exploring the ways and means of bringing forth the voice within each of us. Every paragraph is a treasure.

Andrew Westmoreland
President, Samford University, Birmingham, Alabama

Dr. Smith knows how to preach and shares that know-how by arousing preachers out of timidly approaching doctrinal preaching. It is not dead except it be killed by the "escort" who does not know the steps to the "doxological dance," thereby leading the bride (the church) to be out of "exegetical rhythm" and theologically in doubt. Smith teaches us to meditate—study—wake up and dance, properly "exegeting" the text so as not to destroy the "rhythm" of the dance. I highly endorse *Doctrine That Dances* for required reading in the subject of Christian Preaching. "Let's dance."

Dr. N. Spencer Glover Sr.
Dean of Seminary, Temple Bible College & Seminary, Cincinnati, Ohio

There is about this book a must-read urgency. In the wake of glitzy homiletics that are hourly pumped out over cable and satellite, it is easy to forget there is a huge body of truth that is born in the heart of the Old Testament and erupts in glory from the New. Unless preaching takes root in this deeper soil, the church will shallow out on the God of butterflies and me-dot-com. But Dr. Robert Smith beckons the preacher back to the God who fully disclosed himself in writings of priests and prophets and Jesus Christ. These truths are granite, substantial enough to bear the weight of a concrete value system, that houses a soft, warm, homiletic heart. I challenge you to read your way into this book, just before you preach your way out of it.

Calvin Miller
Professor, Beeson Divinity School, Birmingham, Alabama

Robert Smith is one of the finest preachers of our age, and in his book *Doctrine That Dances* he displays much of the exegetical insight and homiletical passion that make him so effective. Smith demonstrates the urgency of doctrinal preaching for today and offers practical counsel that will help such preaching dance rather than drag.

Michael Duduit
Editor, *Preaching* magazine

Ever since hearing part of this book delivered in a lectureship at our seminary, we have waited expectantly for the full message. Infusing doctrine into preaching, in a day when preaching is so tepid, will contribute to revival in the church and relevance from the pulpit. Doctrinal preaching is not a stale, tired relic from the past. Doctrine dances, and Robert Smith shows us the steps.

Jeff Iorg
President, Golden Gate Seminary

As one appreciates the arduous work of Michelangelo in the Sistine Chapel, so would one laud the literary artistry of Dr. Robert Smith. Passionately and masterfully he paints the preacher's portrait with strokes from biblical mandates, showcasing transparent colors from historical reformers and present colleagues. It is a "must read" for students and scholars, preachers and professors.

Sheila M. Bailey
President, E. K. Bailey Ministries, Dallas, Texas

Whenever Robert Smith preaches, I listen. Whatever Robert Smith writes about preaching, I read. The reason is simple: he is one of God's most consummate communicators—and his preaching is, without doubt, truth through an authentic personality.

James Emery White
President and Professor of Theology and Culture
Gordon-Conwell Theological Seminary

Who doesn't desire to be a better communicator? Dr. Smith will walk you step-by-step to a more dynamic approach of sermon delivery that provides light and fire.

Pastor Johnny Hunt
Woodstock First Baptist Church, Woodstock, Georgia

Smith invites preachers to walk in the footsteps of several biblical characters and become "exegetical escorts" whose job it is to preach in such a way that those who hear the expounding of the Word of God are drawn into an encounter with the Eternal. At the same time, he reminds the preacher that he or she must also be a "doxological dancer" whose sermons should lead people, the preacher included, to offer unending praise to God. The enthusiasm and joy that flow from the preacher can overflow to the congregation. Both of these tasks are made easier for anyone who reads this wonderful book. Let Robert Smith Jr. escort you into the heart and history of preaching. When you have finished this book, you too will most likely become a "doxological dancer."

Marvin A. McMickle, Ph.D.
Professor of Homiletics, Ashland Theological Seminary, Ashland, Ohio

DOCTRINE
That
DANCES

Bringing Doctrinal Preaching and Teaching to Life

Robert Smith Jr.

ACADEMIC

NASHVILLE, TENNESSEE

Published by B&H Publishing Group
Nashville, Tennessee

Dewey Decimal Classification: 230
Subject Heading: PREACHING \ DOCTRINAL THEOLOGY—TEACHING

Unless otherwise indicated, Scripture is quoted from the King James Version. Other versions are identified as follows: Scripture quotations marked HCSB are taken from the *Holman Christian Standard Bible*® Copyright © 1999, 2000, 2002, 2004 by Holman Bible Publishers. Used by permission. ESV, The Holy Bible, English Standard Version, copyright © 2001 by Crossway Bibles, a division of Good News Publishers. Used by Permission. All rights reserved. NASB, the New American Standard Bible, © the Lockman Foundation, 1960, 1962, 1963, 1968, 1971, 1972, 1973, 1975, 1977; used by permission. NIV, unless otherwise noted, Scripture quotations are from the Holy Bible, New International Version, copyright © 1973, 1978, 1984 by International Bible Society. NKJV, New King James Version, copyright © 1979, 1980, 1982, Thomas Nelson, Inc., Publishers. NLT, Scripture quotations marked NLT are taken from the *Holy Bible*, New Living Translation, copyright © 1996. Used by permission of Tyndale House Publishers, Inc., Wheaton, Illinois 60189. All rights reserved. TLB, The Living Bible, copyright © Tyndale House Publishers, Wheaton, Ill., 1971, used by permission. Italic in biblical text has been added by the author for emphasis.

"Fields of Grace," words and music by Darrell Evans, © 2002 Integrity's Hosanna! Music/ASCAP c/o Integrity Media, Inc., 1000 Cody Road, Mobile, AL 36695. All rights reserved. International copyright secured. Used by permission.

"I Hope You Dance," words and music by Tia Sillers and Mark D. Sanders, copyright © 2000 by Choice Is Tragic Music, Ensign Music LLC, Universal Music Corp. and Soda Creek Songs. All rights for Soda Creek Songs controlled and administered by Universal Music Corp. International copyright secured. All rights reserved.

2 3 4 5 6 7 8 9 10 11 12 • 15 14 13 12 11 10 09 08
VP

To my beautiful wife,

Wanda,

who inspires me to dance
in the preaching moment

ACKNOWLEDGMENTS

*I*n the language of Dr. James Earl Massey, this work has been a "burdensome joy." This book reflects the birth pangs of a five-year pregnancy. I am ecstatic that deliverance has finally come, and the burden of writing has given birth to the joy of completion. I am very appreciative to the many persons who walked with me through this reflective journey and helped me finish the race: Dr. George Q. Brown, former pastor, father in the ministry who for nearly fifty years has demonstrated "dancing before the Lord" in his preaching; Dr. N. Spencer Glover, my beloved pastor and confidant; Dr. Timothy George, dean of Beeson Divinity School and cherished friend; Dr. David Dockery, beloved friend and mentor who orchestrated the transition of this writing project from hope to evidence; Dr. James Earl Massey, father in the ministry and "Dad"; Dr. James W. Cox, mentor, friend, and visionary who saw what I did not see—a professorship in preaching—and guided me from vision to reality; Dr. J. Norfleete Day, colleague, beloved sister, and friend whose authentic Christian presence has embodied spiritual formation and nurtured me through the years at Beeson Divinity School; Reverend Freddie T. Piphus Jr., Zion Global Ministries, Cincinnati, Ohio, who afforded me the opportunity to test this writing project during a two-week lecture series at his church in the summer of 2005; Dr. Warren W. Wiersbe, who permitted me to spend a week with him in Lincoln, Nebraska, dialoguing about this work; Denise George, prolific author, encourager, and friend who, in the early stages of this work, provided inspiration and helpful insights and at its completion offered significant counsel; Dr. Calvin Miller, colleague and friend, who motivated me to finish the course; Rev. J. Talbert Prince, precious friend and brother, who provided the presence to see it through; my loving wife, Mrs. Wanda Taylor Smith, whose prayers and dedication to our dual ministry has been the wind underneath my wings; my father, Deacon Robert Smith Sr., who helped to see me through and is waiting for me on the other side; my precious mother, Mrs. Ozella Smith, whose prayers and love have sustained me all of the days of my life; Dr. John Landers, editor and friend, who believed in this writing project and worked to bring it to publication even in his retirement; and to my God who is faithful and true in beginning this work and bringing it to an end. As Paul expressed his appreciation for his helpers in Romans 16, I also give thanks to God for those who have assisted me in typing manuscripts, proofreading texts, and in numerous other literary necessities which enabled an idea to make the transition from the "not yet" to the "already": Rebecca Pounds George, the chief among the amanuenses, Melissa Matthews, Alexis Pigott, Bridget Rose, Rachel "Sophia" Palmer, Brenda L. Harris, Alicia Sanavi, Lark Ball, and Minnie L. Jefferson.

It was my privilege and honor to give lectures in various venues both within and outside of the United State in which I shared many of the concepts that comprise the heart of this book. I am grateful to the leadership of these organizations and institutions that permitted me to lay the foundation for this work: Golden Gate Baptist Theological Seminary, Covenant Theological Seminary, Southern Baptist Theological Seminary, Michigan Baptist State African American Leadership Conference, National Conference on Biblical Preaching, Maryland/Delaware Baptist African American Preachers' Conference, North Carolina Baptist Convention Resource Conference, National Baptist Convention Sunday School and B.T.U. Congress, E. K. Bailey International Expository Preaching Conference, Beeson Divinity School Pastors School, Beeson Divinity School doctrinal preaching classes, Alabama Baptist State Convention, National African American Pastors' Conference, Minnesota/Wisconsin Kingdom Growth Conference, Hampton Ministers' Institute, General Baptist Convention of Texas, Gordon-Conwell Theological Seminary, Dallas Theological Seminary, Southeastern Baptist Theological Seminary, Baptist General Convention of Virginia, Shreveport Ministries Conference, Georgetown College Preachers' Workshop, and International Conference on Preaching, Cambridge, England.

Soli Deo Gloria!
Robert Smith Jr.
May 4, 2007

CONTENTS

DR. JAMES EARL MASSEY

Books which treat the theme and craft of preaching steadily appear, answering the need among preachers for insight, inspiration, and encouragement to handle their perennial task, but books about how to sermonize Christian doctrine are comparatively few and far between. There was a considerable span of years between Henry Sloan Coffin's *What to Preach* (1926) and Andrew W. Blackwood's *Doctrinal Preaching for Today* (1946), or between Merrill R. Abbey's *Living Doctrine in a Vital Pulpit* (1965), William J. Carl III's *Preaching Christian Doctrine* (1984), and Ronald J. Allen's *The Teaching Minister* (1991), all of them works prepared by seasoned and respected practitioners.

By means of the present book, Dr. Robert Smith Jr., himself a seasoned and respected preacher, joins the ranks of those concerned to treat the preaching of doctrine. The insights he has shared here have been gathered from firsthand pulpit responsibilities in a long-term urban pastorate, many engagements as a guest preacher in denominational and ecumenical pulpits, and years of study and reflection and service teaching preaching in a respected divinity school.

Given his background and experience, Dr. Smith has offered something more than theory here, and he has shown both wisdom and warmth in handling his subject so expressively by letting his preaching style both dictate and dominate his expression at so many places in these pages. No overview of his treatment is necessary in this foreword, but it must be stated that the foundational issue that binds these chapters is the importance of preaching doctrine, and to do so in a loving and lively treatment so that it is experienced as an expression of faith and a means to faith.

This book by Dr. Robert Smith Jr. now takes its place among a steadily growing number of resources for those who preach, and rightfully so because the guidance and encouragement it offers can help preachers and their hearers to experience the benefits which essential doctrines embody and make available.

In the introduction he wrote to one of his books about preaching, Charles Haddon Spurgeon (1834–1892), the celebrated Baptist preacher, commented thankfully about the warm reception his first book on the subject had received. Spurgeon wrote: "It is comforting to know that you have aimed at usefulness, pleasant to believe that you have succeeded, and most of all encouraging to have been assured of it by the persons benefited."[1] Robert Smith Jr. has written and released this book with usefulness to preachers as its aim, and I commend it as timely, theologically apt, and readily beneficial.

James Earl Massey
Dean Emeritus and Distinguished Professor-at-Large
Anderson University School of Theology

1 See Charles H. Spurgeon, "Introduction" to *Lectures to My Students* [Second Series] (Grand Rapids: Baker Book House/Guardian Press reprint, 1977).

IS THERE ANY WORD FROM THE LORD?

*T*his book is about doctrinal preaching, about handling biblical truth as the "true and living Word" that it is, with the sermon functioning as a privileged partner with doctrine in what can be described as a joyous doxological dance to the glory of God.

"Therefore what God has joined together, let man not separate" (Matt 19:6 NIV). These are the words of Jesus. Used in the context of preaching, they reflect a critical linkage between *didache* (teaching) and *kerygma* (proclamation). Doctrinal preaching is both content centered (teaching to instruct the mind) and intent centered (preaching to move the heart). Doctrine and joy interpenetrate and are intertwined.

The attitude of the doctrinal preacher must be, "Hallelujah! What a privilege it is to preach about a great God." The truths of Bible doctrine are appropriated, and the preacher serves as a personal witness of those truths because the text of Scripture not only works *on* the preacher but works *in* the preacher as well. The apostle Paul, in 2 Timothy 2:15, admonishes the minister to rightly divide the word of truth. The writer of Hebrews 4:12 speaks of the Word of God as a "two-edged sword" that divides. Ministers who dare to preach doctrinally must always remember that they not only participate in rightly dividing or "cutting straight" the Word of truth before their congregations but that they are also divided by that same Word. Ministers can be guilty of spending much of their time preparing messages that will impact others but not enough time allowing the text of Scripture to impact themselves.

1

Preachers cannot effectively, with the gospel, address people by an intellectual engagement alone. This is exactly what biblical scholar Gerhard von Rad has asserted:

> No understanding at all is possible without some form of inward appropriation. It would be an illusion to think that we could deal with the transmitted intellectual content as a foundry worker handles molten ore with long-handled ladles—and thus keep them at a distance from ourselves. Moreover, no understanding is possible unless what is to be interpreted is applied to ourselves, unless it touches us existentially.[1]

The preacher who handles the Word must first be touched by that same Word. Doctrinal preaching has an impact within both the cognitive and the emotive sectors. Preaching that leaves the cognitive untouched produces hearers who may leave the sanctuary feeling better but without having been helped by the deep doctrinal truths of the Scriptures. Classical rhetoricians attempted to be holistic in the speech act: enlighten the mind, touch the heart, and move the will. Preaching that avoids head engagement will lead to blindness, and preaching that ignores heart engagement—the emotive realm of the believer's existence—does so at the cost of boredom and dullness, which prevents the result of an engaged hearing for a transformed life.

Believers who receive solid doctrinal messages find help to persevere during times of crisis. This is exactly what took place during the period of nazification under Adolph Hitler. The Confessing Church endured persecution and threats under the Nazi regime because their pastors refused to compromise the doctrinal verities of the Bible and proclaimed the Word of God substantively. Pastors like Theophilus Würm, Martin Neimöller, Karl Barth, and Dietrich Bonhoeffer refused to replace the cross with the swastika

1 Gerhard von Rad, *Biblical Interpretation in Preaching*, trans. John Steely (Nashville: Abingdon, 1977), 12.

and Christ with the Führer. Their nonnegotiable creed was, "Jesus is Lord."

Preaching that is not joyous comes across as sterile and is often not received. Dorothy Sayers challenged the thought of many naysayers of her time who claimed that doctrinal preaching led to boredom and a lack of interest. She wrote:

> Official Christianity, of late years, has been having what is known as bad press. We are constantly assured that the churches are empty because preachers insist too much upon doctrine—"dull dogma," as people call it. The fact is the precise opposite. It is the neglect of dogma that makes for dullness. The Christian faith is the most exciting drama that staggered the imagination of man—and the dogma is the drama.[2]

The naysayers were aware, however, that while some actors can read a script based on fiction in such a moving and convincing manner that it becomes real in the minds of the audience, some preachers voice their message in such unconvincing and unpersuasive ways that it comes across as fiction in the minds of the worshippers.

After Peter preached the pentecostal sermon and approximately three thousand people were added to the church, the church continued steadfastly in the apostles' doctrine (Acts 2:42). Let the rocks cry out as an indictment upon us if we fail to pick up the mantle of doctrine!

Does theology exist in order to make preaching as hard as it needs to be? Can the same be asked about doctrine? Doctrine frames and monitors the church's proclamation of the gospel. It also serves as a reservoir from which preaching draws its resources. Doctrinal preaching not only serves as corrective surgery on a congregation; it also offers an element of disease prevention. It

2 Dorothy L. Sayers, "The Greatest Drama Ever Staged," in *Christian Letters to a Post-Christian World* (Grand Rapids: Eerdmans, 1969), 13.

is more than attaching a Band-Aid to a wound; it is also a pro-phylaxis to prevent the affliction. Doctrinal preaching is trifocal in nature. Apologetically, it affirms what is orthodox, or correct, teaching; it contends for "the faith that was once for all entrusted to the saints" (Jude 3 NIV). Apologetics argues for what the church has believed on the basis of God's Word. Polemically, doctrinal preaching stands against false teaching; it sets the church in order when heresies have infected her life. Catechetically, doctrinal preaching nourishes the congregation and thus edifies the body of Christ; the sheep are fed.

From Doctrine to Doxology

Doctrinal preaching serves not only to usher people into the presence of God to learn about Him but also to worship the God who is the object of study. Jesus said to the woman of Samaria, "You worship what you do not know" (John 4:22 ESV). The doctrinal preacher must prevent the church member from engaging in unintelligible worship. The nineteenth-century Danish theologian Søren Kierkegaard critiqued the liturgical model of his national church and many other churches. He argued that God is the audience. C. Welton Gaddy explains:

> Concerned about attitudes toward worship and practices in worship in the churches of his time, Søren Kierkegaard, a nineteenth-century Danish philosopher/theologian, compared what was taking place in the theater and what was happening in Christian worship. In a theater, actors, prompted by people offstage, perform for their audiences. To his dismay, Kierkegaard found that this theatrical model dominated the worship practices of many churches. A minister was viewed as the on-stage actor, God as the offstage prompter, and the congregation as the

audience. Unfortunately, that understanding of worship remains as prevalent as it is wrong.

Each ingredient of the theatrical model mentioned by Kierkegaard is an essential component in Christian worship. Crucial, though, is a proper identification of the role of each one. In authentic worship, the actor is, in fact, many actors and actresses—the members of the congregation. The prompter is the minister, if singular, or, if plural, all of the people who lead in worship (choir members, instrumentalists, soloists, readers, prayers, preachers). The audience is God. Always, without exception, the audience is God!

If God is not the audience in any given service, Christian worship does not take place. If worship does occur and God is not the audience, all present participate in the sin of idolatry.[3]

Preaching is an act of worship. Preaching that simply investigates a body of truth without leading people to worship the God who is truth personified in the person of Jesus misses the mark. Doctrinal preaching desires to bring people into the presence of God, singing,

> Then sings my soul, my Savior, God to Thee;
> How great Thou art, how great Thou art![4]

Doctrine without worship is empty. Worship without doctrine leads to ignorance.

What then shall we say to this matter of doctrinal preaching? What if people remain disinclined about hearing it? What about the reports of killing a church if a consistent diet of doctrine is served from the pulpit? These are some of the questions that

3 C. Welton Gaddy, *The Gift of Worship* (Nashville: Broadman, 1992), 35.
4 Stuart K. Hine, "How Great Thou Art," 1953.

R. W. Dale of Birmingham, England, had to consider when he was interrogated by a minister many years ago. Dale had insisted on preaching doctrinal sermons to his congregation of the Carr's Lane Church. His son, A. W. W. Dale, recorded this pertinent incident:

> One day, soon after he was settled in the pastorate, he met in the streets of Birmingham a congregational minister—a Welshman and a preacher of remarkable power. "He had reached middle age, and I was still a young man, and he talked to me in a friendly way about my ministry. He called: 'I hear that you are preaching doctrinal sermons to the congregation at Carr's Lane; they will not stand it.' I answered: 'They will have to stand it.'"[5]

Ministers who are called by God must preach doctrine even when it is unpopular. Doctrine must be preached because ministers are under divine compulsion and have been given a divine mandate to preach the Word. Paul reminds us that we can be confident in the Word, for "all scripture is given by inspiration of God, and is profitable for doctrine" (2 Tim 3:16). The church of Jesus Christ is often concerned about fanaticism; the greater concern should be about infanticide. Christians are experiencing spiritual immaturity and spiritual death. One of the reasons for this is that worshippers are being served sermonic snacks instead of the doctrinal meat of the Word of God. If doctrine is presented with joy and accuracy, the hearers will not only stand it, they will crave more of it.

I began my work on the idea of this book in 2002. In 2005 I discovered a statement made by Dorothy L. Sayers that confirmed the idea of "doctrine that dances." In a low moment of her life, Sayers' reading of G. K. Chesterton reinforced her faith. In the preface of Chesterton's autobiography, *The Surprise*, Sayers composes

5 A. W. W. Dale, *The Life of R. W. Dale of Birmingham* (London: Hodder and Stoughton, 1902), 108–9.

the words of the preface and pictures Chesterton as a Christian liberator who "like a beneficent bomb . . . blew out of the Church a quantity of stained glass of a very poor period, and let in gusts of fresh air, in which the dead leaves of *doctrine danced* with all the energy and indecorum of Our Lady's Tumbler" (emphasis added).[6]

This Is My Story

As a teenage boy I had the misfortune of not knowing how to dance. I remember giving one of my friends a dollar to teach me. He made a diligent effort but to no avail. As a result, I did not go to community parties or junior high dances after school. I did not even attend our senior high school prom. Although a teenager, I was a preacher, and everyone in my church knew that preachers did not dance. I was attracted to Ian Pitt Watson's work, *A Primer for Preachers*, because in the book I saw a glimpse of my story. In the chapter "Biblical Truth and Biblical Preaching," Watson admitted that as a teenage boy of fourteen, he could not dance. He was awkward and uncoordinated. He missed out on certain social fringe benefits because of his inability to dance. He was envious of his friends who could dance. He decided to master the art of dancing by buying the book *Teach Yourself to Dance* and practicing in private until he perfected his dancing skills. Then he would come out of his privacy and step into the public arena with confidence and coordination. The book contained detailed dance instructions and elaborate diagrams which he learned and memorized. He acknowledged:

> I really knew the book. Intellectually, I had mastered the subject. I also spent many hours trying to put what I knew into practice. I did so alone in my bedroom, using a pillow for a partner and studying my progress in the wardrobe mirror. What I saw in

6 G. K. Chesterton, *The Surprise* (London: Sheed & Ward, 1953), 5.

the mirror was not reassuring! I was putting my feet in all the right places, for I knew the book, and I was doing what the book said. But something was clearly missing. I was thinking the right things and doing the right things, but I couldn't get the feel of it, and in consequence everything I did seemed clumsy—graceless.[7]

Watson said that he attended a party one night and was befriended by a girl who could see that he was having difficulty transferring content into coordination. She invited him to dance with her. He had been accustomed to dancing with a pillow in front of the mirror in his bedroom. Initially, he was quite reluctant to dance because she was so graceful in her movements, and he was so awkward and uncoordinated in his attempts to dance. Finally, he yielded to her invitation. After she began to dance with him, he immediately became aware of a tremendous transformation. He revealed:

> Then something strange happened. A little of her grace seemed to pass to me and I began to get the feel of it. For the first time, all I had learned in the book began to make sense, and even the painful practice in front of the mirror started to pay off. What had been contrived now became natural, what had been difficult now became easy, what had been a burden now became a joy—because at last I had got together what I was thinking and what I was feeling and what I was doing. In that moment I experienced a kind of grace, and it was beautiful.[8]

Preaching is both cranial and cardiological; it involves head and heart, fact and feeling. It is important to proclaim, "Thus

7 Ian Pitt-Watson, *A Primer for Preachers* (Grand Rapids: Baker Academic, 1999), 102.
8 Ibid., 102–3.

saith the Lord." This is the prophetic signature of one sent from God; but one cannot proclaim, "Thus saith the Lord" until that person knows, "What saith the Lord." Once again Watson gives preachers a much-needed and refreshing word that calls for the remarriage of the substance of the text and the style or delivery of the message:

> It comes to us when we get together truth thought, truth felt and truth done. We've got to know the Book; that comes first. And we've got to know what the Book says, follow in Christ's steps. But we can know truth and even do it and still be awkward, inadequate, graceless, until we get the feel of it. That is when we need to remember that it is not meant to be a solo dance. Christ wants us, his church, his clumsy bride, to try it with him. To begin with, we often feel more inadequate than ever when we do that, because we are so awkward and he is so full of grace. Then it happens, in our preaching as in our Christian living. We share in his grace. All the Book says comes alive, and, when we preach it, what used to be contrived now becomes natural, what used to be a labor now becomes spontaneous, what used to be a burden now becomes a blessing, what used to be law now becomes the gospel. Why? Because we are learning the meaning of grace; because now God's truth, thought, felt, and done, is embracing us in the dance—the Truth that stood before Pilate but that Pilate never recognized, because Pilate thought truth was a proposition not a person, a diagram not a dancer.[9]

If preachers doxologically dance as they escort the hearers into the presence of God for the purpose of transformation, they must relinquish their solo sermons and dance with the Savior. The One

---

9 Ibid., 103.

who is full of both grace and truth will teach us to dance doxologically as we escort exegetically. We are invited to follow in His steps (1 Pet 2:21). "The Word became flesh and made his dwelling among us. We have seen his glory, the glory of the One and Only, who came from the Father, full of grace and truth" (John 1:14 NIV).

I received an e-mail from Rebecca Pounds George which further illustrates the truth of John 1:14. The e-mail was titled "Dancing with God":

> When I meditated on the word GUIDANCE, I kept seeing "dance" at the end of the word. I remember reading that doing God's will is a lot like dancing. When two people try to lead, nothing feels right. The movement doesn't flow with the music, and everything is quite uncomfortable and jerky. When one person realizes that, and lets the other lead, both bodies begin to flow with the music. One gives gentle cues, perhaps with a nudge to the back or by pressing lightly in one direction or another. It's as if two become one body, moving beautifully. The dance takes surrender, willingness, and attentiveness from one person and gentle guidance and skill from the other. My eyes drew back to the word GUIDANCE. When I saw "G," I thought of God, followed by "u" and "i." "God 'u' and 'i' dance." God, you and I dance. As I lowered my head, I became willing to trust that I would get guidance about my life. Once again, I became willing to let God lead. My prayer for you today is that God's blessings and mercies be upon you on this day and everyday. May you abide in God as God abides in you. Dance together with God, trusting God to lead and to guide you through each season of your life. . . . And I hope you dance!!![10]

10 Anonymous e-mail received on November 9, 2004 by Rebecca Pounds George.

Chapter One

TOWARD A DEFINITION OF DOCTRINAL PREACHING

*T*he late Jaroslav Pelikan, the celebrated historical theologian, stated, "What the church of Jesus
Christ believes, teaches and confesses on the basis
of the Word of God: this is Christian doctrine."[1] Peter Toon, in
an insightful treatment of the development of doctrine across the
history of the church, explained doctrine as "a historically conditioned response of the Church to questions put to her at a particular time and place by the world or by her members."[2] However,
we can define doctrine more easily than we can define doctrinal
preaching. One of the ways of attempting a definition of doctrinal
preaching is to show the relationship that doctrine has to preaching. William J. Carl III provides a clear portrait of the association
of doctrine with preaching. He contends that:

> Doctrine is not identical with the proclamation of the
> gospel. Doctrine serves proclamation, enriches and
> enlarges it, largely in a critical role, as a criterion for
> determining that what the church proclaims today is
> in harmony with scripture and its tradition, that it is
> truly human language about God and not about the
> latest spiritual trend or social ethical passion.[3]

In conjunction with doctrine's critical relationship to preaching,
like an arbiter or umpire of a baseball game who demands that

---

1 Jaroslav Pelikan, *The Christian Tradition: A History of the Development of Doctrine*, vol. 1 (Chicago: University of Chicago Press, 1971), 1.
2 Peter Toon, *The Development of Doctrine in the Church* (Grand Rapids: Eerdmans, 1979), 81.
3 William J. Carl III, "Doctrine," in *Concise Encyclopedia of Preaching*, ed. William H. Willimon and Richard Lischer (Louisville: Westminster John Knox,
1995), 102.

the game be played according to the rules of the baseball manual, doctrine insists that preaching be carried out in harmony with the regulations of the biblical manual.

Furthermore, Carl discerns the affiliation that the rules of English grammar have with ordinary English conversation in light of the relationship that doctrine has with preaching. He quotes George Lindbeck, who said, "There is a parallel intimate relationship between the rules of English grammar and ordinary American discourse."[4] Carl further argues:

> Not all discourse that employs Christian vocabulary is proper Christian discourse any more than a sentence using nothing but English terms, such as "He don't do no wrong to nobody," qualifies as a proper English sentence. . . . We have come to recognize its impropriety as a result of our mastery of English grammar and our use of these rules to criticize and evaluate the sentence. In much the same way, Christian doctrines should function to criticize discourse that flows from the pulpit. . . . Preachers need to concern themselves with doctrine, then, in every sermon that they preach, just as authors need to attend to grammatical rules when writing. Just as the rules of subject-verb agreement inform the writing of this paragraph, so the Trinity doctrine must inform the way preachers speak when referring to God as Father, Son, and Holy Spirit, reminding them that their discourse does not imply that Christians believe in three gods.[5]

While preachers know what doctrinal preaching is, it is difficult to articulate succinctly what it is in one descriptive and pregnant sentence. A definition is a limitation. Once something is

4 George Lindbeck, "The Nature of Doctrine," in *Concise Encyclopedia of Preaching*, 102–3.
5 Carl, "Doctrine," 103.

defined, there is the inevitability of leaving something important out of the definition.

We live in a communication-crazed community. Words, words, and more words! Left-brained people especially emphasize the value of words. Warren W. Wiersbe asks, "How do you define life and taste? How do you give a definition for the essence of the feeling of being in love?" He cites the poet Walt Whitman, who once listened to a lecture of a learned astronomer who discussed the meticulous matters of the universe and the relationship of the bodily elements of space. After growing weary of this technical, scientific lecture, Whitman went out and looked at the stars![6]

People want preachers to define everything for them, and they are sometimes disappointed when the preachers tell them that they are unable to do so. Some things are enveloped within the realm of what Rudolf Otto called the *mysterium tremendum*, or the tremendous mystery. Some things have to be experienced. In a way, doctrinal preaching can only be approached in an effort to define itself because the essence and reality of doctrinal preaching is bigger than any definition. Doctrinal preaching is not a mechanical process governed by a human agent; rather, it is an event that happens under the auspices of the Holy Spirit who reveals the doctrinal truths and testifies of the person of Christ. Consequently, doctrinal preaching is shrouded in mystery. In an attempt to define doctrinal preaching, the mystery cannot be demystified, and the inscrutable cannot be scrutinized.

We can only move toward a definition of doctrinal preaching. We are on the way without any possibility of ever fully arriving! While it is true that we must experience the essence of doctrinal preaching, we must also know what we are experiencing. Among the many qualities of the effectiveness of Paul as a doctrinal preacher was his conviction about what he preached and who he preached about. He reminded Timothy that all Scripture is God breathed and is profitable for doctrine (2 Tim 3:16). Scripture is

6 Conversation with Warren W. Wiersbe, August 9, 2004, Lincoln, NE.

just as God breathed as the body of Adam that received the breath of God; Scripture is just as God breathed as the corpses in the valley of dry bones that became a resuscitated army when the *ruach*, or breath of God, was breathed into them. Because Paul had this confidence, he could exclaim, "For I know *whom* I have believed, and am persuaded that he is able to keep that which I have committed unto him against that day" (2 Tim 1:12).

We are challenged by 1 Peter 3:15 to "be ready always to give an answer to every man that asketh you a reason of the hope that is in you." Growing up in the church of my childhood, the Rose Chapel Missionary Baptist Church in Cincinnati, Ohio, the senior choir would sing the choral rendition, "It's Real," and do so with great passion and confidence. I can still see the streams of tears running down the eyes of those senior saints, and I can still hear both men and women shouting as they waved their hands in personal witness to the truth of the lyrics of the song: "Yes, yes, I know it's real." I am convinced that these lyrics must undergird the sermonic statements of our doctrinal preaching.

> O how well do I remember how I doubted day by day,
> For I did not know for certain that my sins were washed away.
> When the Spirit tried to tell me, I the truth would not receive;
> I endeavored to be happy and to make myself believe.
> . . . .
> But at last I tired of living such a life of fear and doubt,
> For I wanted God to give me something I would know about;
> So the truth would make me happy and the light would clearly shine,

And the Spirit gave assurance that I'm His and He
is mine.

. . . .

So I prayed to God in earnest; and not caring what
folks said,
I was hungry for the blessing; my poor soul—it must
be fed.
Then at last by faith I touched him and, like sparks
from smitten steel,
Just so quick salvation reached me. O bless God I
know it's real!

Chorus

It's real, it's real,
O I know it's real
Praise God the doubts are settled
For I know, I know, it's real.[7]

Doctrine has a subservient role to preaching. While doctrine
may exist to make preaching as disciplined as it needs to be, doctrine's mission is to be a servant to proclamation. Doctrine's purpose is not merely to be derived, constructed, and formalized and
to remain in the archives of academia for scholarly use only. Rather,
doctrine is the possession of the church and must be preached.
Preaching extracts its communicative strength from the reservoirs
of doctrine and draws its riches from the wells of its truths. The
doctrine behind and below the sermon gives it stability.

As Narcissus saw his reflection in a pool of water, so doctrine
ought to see its image in the face of preaching. It gives the sermon
its shape. After the sermon is preached, the hearers may not initially recognize an identifiable doctrine within the sermon because
the preacher may have expounded on the doctrine of sanctification
without ever using the word *sanctification* during the preaching
event. But the hearer ought to be able to detect the image behind

7 Homer L. Cox, "It's Real," 1907.

the doctrine and arrive at the intended doctrinal experience. It is better to experience repentance, joy, and justification than merely to learn about them.

I do not have in mind the lessening of the importance of knowing doctrine; I just want to remind preachers constantly that doctrinal preaching not only informs our learning but also influences our living. We can never "fully know" during our terrestrial trek. Paul was right, "Now we see through a glass, darkly; but *then* face to face: *now* we know in part; but *then* I shall know even as also I am known" (1 Cor 13:12). But *then*! When the terrestrial trek is terminated and the celestial course is initiated, the "now-ness" of time will, in the words of the inimitable Dr. Gardner C. Taylor, fall exhausted at the feet of the "then-ness" of eternity. Not only will we have "no less days to sing God's praise," but we will also have no less days to learn more fully about the One to whom doctrine points.

We have heard about the love of God over the years, but after being in the presence of the Lord for a million years, we will only know just a little bit more of what the unconditional love of God really is. We have studied about the atonement for sin for a long period of time, but after staring at the nail prints in the Lord's hands for a billion years and gazing at the Lamb that was slain for our redemption, we will know only a smidgen of what the atonement really means. We have thought long and hard about the holiness of God, and reminded our congregants, "Be ye holy; for I am holy" (1 Pet 1:16). But after a trillion years we will know only a fraction about the holiness of God that causes angels to cover their feet and faces and to fly away as they sing a song that reverberates throughout the corridors of heaven, earth, and hell: "Holy, holy, holy is the LORD of hosts; the whole earth is full of his glory" (Isa 6:3).

Consider a scene where a seagull is dispatched every year and flies to the Rock of Gibraltar, where it brushes its beak against that granite rock formation and flies away only to return a thousand years later. If that process is repeated every thousand years until the Rock of Gibraltar is reduced to sea level, in comparison, we would have only been in heaven for a day. There will never be a moment in time or eternity in which we will fully comprehend the doctrines of the Bible that we preach. What Phillips Brooks told students at Yale still holds true: "Preach doctrine, preach all the doctrine you know, and learn forever more and more; but preach it always, not that men may believe it, but that men may be saved by believing it."[8] Exegesis must be combined with experience, deeds must be merged with doctrine, lips must be linked to lives, and beliefs must be integrated with behavior.

Charles Bugg referred to Phillips Brooks' assertion, which compared the Bible to a telescope. The telescope is not designed to look *at* but to look *through*, to see that which is beyond us.[9] Additionally, Bugg cited the comment of Robert McCracken, who, while senior minister of the Riverside Church in New York City, was asked by someone why people kept coming to Riverside to hear his sermons. McCracken replied, "They keep coming hoping to hear a word from beyond themselves."[10]

Dr. Greg Thornbury, a professor at Union University in Jackson, Tennessee, interviewed Dr. Carl F. H. Henry, founding editor of *Christianity Today*, shortly before Henry died. Thornbury asked him what was the most profound question he had ever put to his students. Dr. Henry bypassed the conundrum of catechesis, the intricacies of systematic theology, and the profundity of doctrinal explanation and stated, "The most profound question I have ever asked my students is, 'Have you ever met the risen Lord?'"[11] This question goes beyond the mere recitation of a creed, the explanation of a doctrine, or the clarification of a biblical regulation. It points to a relationship with the person of Jesus Christ. Doctrinal preaching must move from merely learning *biblical regulations*, or

8 Phillips Brooks, *Lectures on Preaching* (Grand Rapids: Zondervan, 1950), 129.
9 Charles Bugg, "Back to the Bible: Toward a New Description of Expository Preaching," *Review and Expositor* 90 (1993): 414.
10 Ibid.
11 Gregory Alan Thornbury, "Carl F. H. Henry: Heir of Reformation Epistemology," *Southern Baptist Journal of Theology* 8 (2004): 62–74.

the indication that we cannot live holy, as God requires. It must move toward *gospel revelation*, for Christ enables us to do what we cannot do—to live holy! Ultimately it must move to forging a *relationship* with Christ. For Dr. Henry it was not just a matter of testing a student on the historical claims of the resurrection of Jesus; his ultimate concern was whether the student had an experiential encounter with the Lord.

Job did not give a lecture on the person of the Redeemer; instead he declared, "I know that my Redeemer lives" (Job 19:25 NIV). The blind man in John 9 did not need a seminar on blindness; he needed his sight. He declared, "Whereas I was blind, now I see" (John 9:25). People who come to hear us on Sunday morning do not merely need more *information* about Bible facts; they need *transformation*. This is why Harry Emerson Fosdick penned the classic line nearly eighty years ago, "Only the preacher proceeds still upon the idea that folk come to church desperately anxious to discover what happened to the Jebusites."[12] They come to have the tragedies and struggles in their lives addressed from the perspective of a God who is able to change their situations and/or to give them strength to endure them with joy. Doctrine, in its association with preaching, epitomizes the role that salt plays in protecting meat from decay. Doctrine is the protector of preaching. Without it preaching would fall into heresy.

Additionally, doctrine is inseparably and inextricably integrated with true preaching and promotes the development and health of proclamation. Like yeast, which loses itself in dough and yet causes the dough to graduate from flatness to a fully rounded dinner roll, doctrine causes preaching to rise in fullness of authority and accent. Doctrine offers a moral conscience to preaching that prevents preaching from giving all of its attention to the heights of heaven while ignoring the social inequities on earth. Doctrine confronts preaching with this truth: "These things should have

12 Edmund Holt Linn, *Preaching as Counseling* (Valley Forge, PA: Judson, 1966), 92.

18

been done without neglecting the others" (Matt 23:23 HCSB). Jesus confronted the Pharisees with their boast concerning tithing and stated that yes, they should have tithed, but they also should not have neglected the matters of social justice. The moral conscience of doctrine makes arrangements for preaching to meet at the intersection of the vertical relationship between God and humans and the horizontal relationship between humans and humans. This moral conscience of doctrine insists that preachers be acquainted not only with the streets of gold in heaven but also with the streets of gloom in the ghetto. It unites the pulpit and the pavement, the sanctuary and the street, Bethlehem and Birmingham, the New Jerusalem and New Jersey.

Doctrine relates to preaching in the same manner that John the Baptist related to Jesus. When John the Baptist received news that Jesus was baptizing more persons than he was baptizing, John did not assume the posture of a competitor because his ministry was one of negation: he was neither the light nor the Christ. Rather, he was the best man alongside Jesus, the bridegroom. His job was to focus on the bridegroom and in the process, John the Baptist, the best man, would decrease while Jesus, the bridegroom, would increase (John 3:30). Preaching that lacks doctrine is anemic and weak. The preaching of Bible doctrine, however, is preaching that is powerful and effective.

Definitions of expository preaching provided by some of the great voices in preaching furnish assistance in the endeavor to define doctrinal preaching. They aid us in moving toward an operative definition that illustrates the positive intention and focus of this book. E. K. Bailey, late pastor of Concord Baptist Church in Dallas, Texas, and founder of the E. K. Bailey International Expository Preaching Conference, defines expository preaching as "a message that focuses on a portion of scripture so as to clearly establish the precise meaning of the text, and to poignantly motivate the hearers to actions or attitudes dictated by that text in the power of the Holy Spirit."[13] Like expository preaching, doctrinal preaching is consistent with the text out of which the doctrine emerges. Preachers who would preach doctrinally must put their ears to the pavement of the text and synchronize the heartbeat of the text with the heartbeat of the doctrine so that the author's intention is clearly seen and heard. Doctrinal preachers preach with passion and conviction, attempting to persuade the hearers to embrace the mind-set and the behavior prescribed by the doctrine in the text. Preachers who would preach the doctrine in the text must stand with Martin Luther, John Calvin, and others in the Reformation heritage who believed that when they were accurately speaking in accordance to the Word of God, Christ is speaking.[14]

Haddon Robinson, staunch homiletician at Gordon-Conwell Theological Seminary near Boston, Massachusetts, penned his classic definition of expository preaching (used interchangeably with biblical preaching):

> Expository preaching is the communication of a biblical concept transmitted through a historical, grammatical, and literary study of a passage in its context, which the Holy Spirit first applies to the personality and experience of the preacher, then through him to his hearers.[15]

These words ring true to preachers of Bible doctrine. The preacher must lift doctrine out of a passage instead of infusing a passage with foreign doctrine. Doctrinal preachers must also pay close attention to the grammatical elements of the original biblical languages in the passage. An examination of John 20:5–8 will reveal that there are three different Greek words for sight in the passage. In John 20:5, John "sees" the linen cloths as he stoops

13 E. K. Bailey, *Ten Reasons for Expository Preaching* (Dallas, TX: E. K. Bailey Ministries, 2003), 2:1.
14 See also Luke 10:16.
15 Haddon W. Robinson, *Biblical Preaching* (Grand Rapids: Baker, 1980), 20.

down and looks in from outside the sepulcher. In the Greek the word is *blepei* (he saw), which indicates a casual glance. John 20:6 indicates that Peter goes inside the sepulcher and also "sees" the linen cloths. The word for "see" in this instance is *theorei* (he saw), which expresses a more thoughtful and calculated look. Finally, in John 20:8, John goes inside the sepulcher the second time, "sees," and believes. In the Greek the word for "sees" in this case is *eiden* (he saw), which conveys belief. Could these three distinct Greek words suggest the stages of faith through which some people process before experiencing mature faith?

Preachers of Christian doctrine must also attend to the historical details in the passage. For example, is the teaching from a passage applicable for a specific time, place, and people, or for all times, places, and all peoples? The literary study of the genre of a particular passage should always be taken into account. The book of Proverbs is the inspired word of God, but it is not a book of guarantees. Much harm has been done by preachers who have preached Proverbs 22:6 with a sense of guarantee: "Train up a child in the way he should go: and when he is old, he will not depart from it." Many parents have incriminated themselves because their children departed from their Christian upbringing and teaching. Since the preacher proclaimed the text as a guarantee, the parents felt that they were evidently lacking in their parenting because their children did not lead exemplary Christian lives. However, this interpretation would seem to contradict the situation of Josiah, the godly king of Judah, who had an evil father (Amon), a wicked grandfather (Manasseh), and a righteous great-grandfather (Hezekiah). The book of Proverbs states the principles that, when embraced, generally will give expected results.

This text really says that children will not depart from the "way" because the "way," or the "teaching," is in them. The prodigal son came back home to his father not because he attended a revival and was convicted of his waywardness but because the "way," or the "teaching," of his father remained in him. Like a medicinal time-released capsule, the "way" began to speak to him in the pigpen, and he went home with a different attitude than the one he had when he left home. Christian parents whose children have departed from the teachings they were exposed to in their home need to cease punishing themselves and emulate the father of the prodigal son who kept the calf fattened in expectation of the return of the son.[16]

Preachers of Christian doctrine contemplate the context of the text, looking at it in light of the chapter of the particular book, the purpose of the book, its relationship to the particular testament, and even its role within the entire canon of Scripture. Doctrinal preachers recognize that the Holy Spirit, the actual preacher, preaches to them before they preach to their congregations. The Spirit applies the doctrinal message to the preacher's life and personality and then to the hearers'.

The renowned Anglican preacher-theologian John R. W. Stott asserts that expository preaching is "the opening up of the inspired text with such faithfulness and sensitivity that God's voice is heard and His people obey Him."[17] Stott is convinced of this and contends that preachers of Bible doctrine possess at least these two convictions: first, they are firm in their conviction that the Bible is not *a* word of God, but *the* Word of God that is inspired and God breathed. They are also firm in their conviction that the Bible is a closed book that must be opened by the Holy Spirit and the truth rightly divided, or "cut straight," by the preacher (see 2 Tim 2:15).

There are also at least two obligations of doctrinal preachers. They must be faithful to the text of Scripture, and they must be sensitive to the hearers. In reality they not only exegete the text, but they also exegete the hearers.

Finally, doctrinal preachers have at least two expectations. If they are accurate in delivering the doctrinal message, then they

16 Luke 15:23.
17 Given at a conference on expository preaching.

can expect God's Word to be heard, although, like Isaiah who cried out, "Who hath believed our report?" they wonder if it is believed (Isa 53:1). They can also expect the people to obey God because His Word will get a hearing whether it is heard immediately or futuristically, in compliance or disobedience; His Word will not return to Him void (Isa 55:11).

Although doctrinal preaching is difficult to define, William J. Carl III offers what appears to be the fullest possible definition:

> Doctrinal preaching, then, is Christian preaching grounded in the biblical witness to Jesus Christ; it starts with text, doctrine, or cultural question, but tends to focus on one or more Christian doctrines regardless of its starting point.[18]

In connection with Carl, doctrinal preachers locate the center of Bible doctrine not in a proposition but in the person of Jesus Christ. As Jesus admonished that the Scriptures be searched because they testify of Him (John 5:39), preachers of Christian doctrine make Christ the heart of their preaching. If the Bible is read backwards, one will see that Jesus Christ, the Lamb of God, was slain from the foundation of the world (Rev 13:8). This means that in the mind of God, Calvary was a forethought and not an afterthought. God did not react to the fall of Adam and Eve, but rather He pre-acted *before* the fall of Adam and Eve. The Old Testament proclaimed that Christ is coming. The New Testament announced that Christ has come and will come again.

Doctrinal preaching might begin with a text, especially if the preacher is preaching a sermonic series through a book of the Bible. It could start with a doctrine, such as an article in the Apostles' Creed, which is a summary or compendium of truths that the church believes and espouses. Or it could commence with a relevant cultural question. Paul Tillich often charged the church with answering questions that no one was asking. Doctrinal preachers

18 William J. Carl III, *Preaching Christian Doctrine* (Philadelphia: Fortress, 1984), 8–9.

23

must pay attention to the questions voiced by culture. For example, in late December 2004, tsunamis, gigantic tidal waves caused by an earthquake and the shifting of plates under the ocean, cost more than 150,000 persons their lives in Southeast Asia. Many American citizens were there as tourists, and a number of them lost their lives. The tsunamis not only ravaged the land but left people injured, separated from families, without food and clean water, and exposed to rampant and advancing disease. The overall question on the minds of those who come to church to hear us is, "Why?" The doctrinal preacher must address this question of theodicy. Sometimes the only thing we can do after speaking to this matter is to lead inquiring people to Calvary and encourage them to hear anew and ponder again the words of Jesus, "My God, my God, why . . . ?" (Mark 15:34).

But we must not leave them with this question. They must be challenged to persevere through the mist of mystery and make the commitment of Jesus, "Father, into thy hands" (Luke 23:46). Doctrinal preaching does not answer all the questions and cannot solve all the problems, but it points the listeners to God, who is sovereign yet suffers with us in our stricken situations. The Lord is not removed from human plight; He is the Immanuel on our Emmaus road. We do not subscribe to the teaching of anti-patripassianism, the doctrine that teaches that God is removed from pain and the sharing of human suffering. The Lord suffers with us. As our high priest, He can be touched with the feeling of our infirmities (Heb 4:15). Doctrinal preachers punctuate Carl's thought that regardless of the starting point, doctrinal preaching will tend to focus on one or more Christian doctrines. Doctrine is found in life, and life is found in doctrine.

How then is doctrinal preaching to be defined? As Haddon Robinson stated, "Defining becomes sticky business because what we define we sometimes destroy. . . . Preaching is a living process involving God, the preacher, and the congregation, and no definition can pretend to capture that dynamic. But we must attempt a working definition anyway."[19]

My definition of doctrinal preaching emphasizes its underlying aim: transformation through Christ. I state that doctrinal preaching is *the escorting of the hearers into the presence of God for the purpose of transformation.* I contend that the task of the doctrinal preacher is to serve as an escort who ushers the hearer into the presence of God through the proper and precise expounding of the Word of God. When this is done, the efforts of doctrinal preachers have reached their limits because they cannot transform the hearer. The hearer is left in the presence of the only One who can transform a human soul—Christ. Preachers of Christian doctrine may inform the hearer's mind, which in turn serves to direct one to Christ, but only Christ can transform the hearer's heart.

The operational definition of doctrinal preaching is *the magnifying of Jesus Christ through the explanation and application of the basic truths of the Christian faith.* Doctrinal preaching must have an object. We cannot have faith in faith; we do not worship worship; and doctrine cannot exist for doctrine's sake. Doctrinal preaching carries out the mission of magnifying Jesus Christ. To magnify Jesus Christ is not literally to make Him bigger. His influence is already felt in three worlds: heaven, earth, and hell. Heaven is His throne, and the earth is His footstool. He fills the universe with His power. Rather, to magnify Christ through doctrinal preaching is to present Him in such a way that the hearers see Him in a more glorious, majestic, holy, sovereign, just, faithful, and mighty manner than they have ever seen Him before. This is made possible when the preacher of Christian doctrine, through the power of the Spirit, explains the basic and fundamental truths of the Christian faith and shows how they apply to the Christian life. Consequently, the function of doctrinal preaching is to ferry the truths of the "was-ness" of the Word from the shore of the ancient text to the shore of the "is-ness" of our contemporary world.

19 Robinson, *Biblical Preaching,* 19.

Chapter Two

A METAPHORICAL RATIONALE FOR
DOCTRINAL PREACHING

hese are difficult times for preachers to accept the reality that words, particularly abstract words, are oftentimes not enough. Some things cannot be expressed with words. Richard Lischer, Yale Beecher preaching lecturer, addresses this matter in his engaging book *The End of Words.*[1] Dietrich Bonhoeffer said: "The time when people could be told everything by means of words, whether theological or pious is over."[2] Some realities and emotions are just too deep for words. Words cannot express the emotions of tears running down a child's eyes upon learning that his or her parents have survived the tsunami in Southeast Asia in December 2004. Tears represent liquid love, a language that both God and people understand. The psalmist says that God takes our tears and puts them in a bottle against the day of remembrance (Ps 56:8). Tears testify to the trials that believers experience. Paul acknowledges, "We do not know what we ought to pray for, but the Spirit himself intercedes for us with groans that words cannot express" (Rom 8:26 NIV). Some realities and emotions cannot be expressed in words; some things are too deep for words.

To hear the surgeon say on the morning following the operation, "We got all of it!"; to watch a bride walking down the aisle on that long-awaited wedding day; to see a young man come forward during the close of the Sunday worship experience and then testify that God has set him free from drug addiction and to thank the church community for praying during the period

---

1 Richard Lischer, *The End of Words* (Grand Rapids: Eerdmans, 2005).
2 Dietrich Bonhoeffer, *Letters and Papers from Prison*, trans. Reginald Fuller, Frank Clark, et al., ed. Eberhard Bethge (1953; repr., New York: Simon & Schuster, 1997), 279, 329, 360.

of his chemical dependency; to receive an envelope containing the semester's grades, to focus slowly on the grade that you were most concerned about and discover that you scored higher in that course than you could have imagined; to be bathed in God's grace and to bask in God's blessings while recognizing that you are utterly unworthy—there are some things, some experiences, and some events that are too deep for words. In his book *God Came Near*, Max Lucado refers to Jesus' miracle in healing a man who could not hear and who had a speech impediment. Jesus spat on the ground and applied the spittle to the man's tongue and ear. Before he pronounced the opening of the man's ear and the loosing of the man's tongue, Jesus *sighed*! Lucado interprets that sigh as His wordless expression: "It was never intended to be this way."[3] There are some things that are too deep for words to capture.

James Weldon Johnson's *Lift Every Voice and Sing* captures this wordless expression designed to articulate inferentially the desire of the Negro people for freedom and racial equality:

> Stony the road we trod, bitter the chastening rod,
> Felt in the day when hope unborn had died.
> Yet with a steady beat, have not our weary feet,
> Come to the place for which our fathers *sighed*.[4]

There are some things that are too deep for words to capture.

Francis of Assisi is reported to have said to his disciples, "Preach the gospel at all times and, when necessary, use words."[5] It is true that a sermon *seen* has more quality than one that is simply *heard*. There are some things that are too deep for words.

---

3 Max Lucado, *God Came Near* (Sisters, OR: Multnomah, 1986), 61; cp. Mark 7:34.
4 James Weldon Johnson, 1921.
5 Attributed to St. Francis of Assisi, http://www.livingcatholicism.com/archives/2005/04/simple_ways_to.html, accessed May 15, 2007.

Blaise Pascal stated, "The heart knows the reason that reason knows not of."[6] There are some things that you know without the benefit of articulation. These things are too elastic and too deep for words to capture.

In his autobiography, *Notes from a Wayfarer*, Helmut Thielicke said, "The nose is the organ for unconscious memories."[7] The nose assists us in making the inexpressible expressible by recalling an experience through the stimulation of a certain aroma. Certain smells will take your mind back to certain places. Grandma's kitchen and the baking of chocolate chip cookies. The perfume a young man gave his first girlfriend. The paper mill outside the city limits. All of these fleeting smells can evoke memories. "Precious memories, how they linger!"

As the Old Testament scholar Walter Brueggemann said in *Finally Comes the Poet*, "To address the issue of a truth greatly reduced requires us to be poets who speak against a prose world."[8] Some things are just too deep and evasive for words. If something is false in the mind, the preacher who has a discerning mind understands that what is wrong in Scripture cannot be right in the heart. And this should be our checkpoint. It is not enough to get emotionally excited in the heart. The mind says look at the text; there has to be consistency. If it's right in the mind, then it will be right in the heart.

Paul says that we are to pray in the Spirit and with understanding, sing in the Spirit and with understanding. Should not preachers preach in the Spirit (heart) and with understanding (mind)? There must be consistency in the head and the heart. The preacher must make the longest journey in homiletical history—the eighteen-inch distance between the head and the heart—in

6 Blaise Pascal, *Pensées: The Provincial Letters* (New York: Modern Library, 1941), 95.
7 Helmut Thielicke, *Notes from a Wayfarer*, trans. David R. Law (New York: Paragon, 1995), 2.
8 Walter Brueggemann, *Finally Comes the Poet* (Minneapolis: Fortress, 1980), 3.

order to maintain this connection and consistency and prevent contradiction.

Metaphors speak to the heart. Sometimes truth is first experienced before it is taught and reflected upon. Then one begins to systematize and organize truth in order to reinforce what is experienced.

How do we present truth? Orally, through what we hear? Visually, through what we see? Emotionally, through what we feel? We present truth tridimensionally through what we hear, see, *and* feel. The gospel is inspired—"All Scripture is given by inspiration of God" (2 Tim 3:16). But the gospelizer who carries the gospel is *perspired*. Something happens to the carriers as they share the gospel. It is not just what they see, hear, or feel; it is all three dimensions.

Just Right for Images

How do words adequately express regret, love, hope, loss, peace, and joy? When words fall exhausted at the feet of futility, another medium has to be used to translate human experience and expression. This medium is metaphorical language that speaks through "silent pictures." The nineteenth-century Danish philosopher Søren Kierkegaard wrote of a traveling circus known as the Medici. The workers would set up the stage, and during one of the acts, they would set the stage ablaze in a fabulous fireworks exhibition before extinguishing it. One day, while the circus performers were getting dressed for the next show, an actual fire broke out. The only performer who was dressed was the clown. He was sent to the city to recruit citizens to bring buckets of water and help put out the fire. Because he was dressed like a clown, the citizens did not take his request seriously. When he pointed to the smoke ascending in the area of the circus tent, they immediately went with the clown and assisted in extinguishing the fire. The clown's words did not engage the citizens. It was only when he pointed to a clear, undeniable picture that they were motivated to put out the fire.[9]

In the acclaimed movie *A Time to Kill*, a white lawyer appeals to a white jury to exonerate a black man who killed two white men who raped his daughter. Propositions had failed to move the jury in his favor. He appealed to their imagination and asked the jury to close their eyes and imagine a little girl being raped, her womb destroyed so that she would have no reproductive future, blood and semen splattered over her body, hung on a tree limb and her body pounded with thrown beer cans and eventually thrown in a ditch. Then, the lawyer said, "Imagine that she was white." The jury's verdict was "not guilty."[10] A picture triumphed over a proposition.

An image wrongly used gives people the wrong message, which causes people to respond inappropriately. Thus, the right metaphors, pictures, and images are essential. It is true that a picture is worth a thousand words. During the preaching moment in the African American church, it is not uncommon to hear worshippers say, "Paint the picture, Doc," in response to picturesque preaching. Before the days of visual technology, the black preacher who often could not read the text could paint so vividly the picture of Joshua and the battle of Jericho that the worshippers could *see* the walls tumbling down. Black preachers could describe so clearly what they saw in the text that the hearers could vividly see the biblical image.

The Ministry of the Metaphor

A metaphor is an extension of meaning through the comparison of one thing to another. *Webster's New World Dictionary* defines a metaphor as "a figure of speech containing an implied comparison,

9 Søren Kierkegaard, *Either/Or Part 1* (Princeton, NJ: Princeton University Press, 1987), 30.
10 *A Time to Kill*, dir. Joel Schumacher, perf. Matthew McConaughey, Samuel L. Jackson, Sandra Bullock, DVD, Regency Enterprises, 1996.

in which a word or phrase ordinarily and primarily used for one thing is applied to another." One of the great metaphors in the Bible is found in Genesis 48. Jacob is practically blind and does not expect to see his son Joseph again. When he is informed that Joseph has arrived to see him, he sits up in the bed, excited. He is overjoyed to learn that Joseph has not come alone but rather has brought his two sons, Manasseh and Ephraim, to see their grandfather. Joseph has brought them in order to adhere to a family custom in which Jacob will bless his grandsons. In this custom Jacob would stand in the place of God and pronounce this blessing upon these boys, believing that God would bring the blessing to pass even after Jacob dies.

Joseph places the older son, Manasseh, on the right side of the bed and positions the younger son, Ephraim, on the left side of the bed, and waits for Jacob to place his hands upon them and pronounce the blessing. This particular hand placement ensures that the older Manasseh receives the greater blessing and the younger Ephraim receives the lesser blessing. So as not to entrust the hand placement to Jacob's failing sight, Joseph himself positions Jacob's hands.

Many years earlier, Jacob had taken advantage of his own father's failing sight and deceived his father into erroneously giving him the testamentary blessing. Now he chose to depart from traditional protocol and crossed his hands, thus placing his right hand on the younger Ephraim and his left hand on the older Manasseh. Joseph protested. He knew that the right hand was the hand of power. Since this was the case, upon the birth of Jacob's twelfth son, Jacob changed his name to "Benjamin," meaning "the son of my right hand" (Gen 35:18).

There are other biblical images relating to the right hand. Jesus ascended to heaven after He finished His earthly labor and sat down at the right hand of God (Heb 12:2). Similarly, while Stephen was being stoned, he prayed and saw Jesus standing at the right hand of God (Acts 7:55). The apostle John saw the glorified Christ holding the seven stars in His right hand (Rev 1:16).

31

The crossing of Jacob's hands speaks of God's sovereignty in bypassing human tradition and custom so that the divine design and plan may be executed. This metaphor speaks to the pain predicament in human crises. God turns hindrances into helps, interruptions into invitations, problems into possibilities, stress into strength, and tragedy into triumph.

Jesus used metaphors throughout his ministry by comparing one thing to another in order to establish his thought. Jesus warned against placing new wine into old wineskins (Luke 5:37). He knew that old wineskins, having been stretched to their capacity, are brittle and no longer supple. If unfermented wine is put into unstretchable wineskins, the fermentation activity will burst the wineskins, and both wine and wineskins will be lost. Through this metaphor, Jesus asserted that the wineskins of law and traditional religion must be changed to accommodate the new wine of the gospel of grace. The new wine takes believers from grace to grace and from glory to glory. The law came by Moses, but grace and truth came through Jesus Christ. In the spirit of the Negro spiritual "We Are Climbing Jacob's Ladder," every round goes higher, higher. God is preparing believers by expanding their capacity to receive God's ability as they yield their availability.

Herod Antipas, the governor of Galilee who executed John the Baptist, thought that John the Baptist had risen from the dead in the person of Jesus. When Herod Antipas asked Jesus to perform a miracle for his own pleasure and entertainment, Jesus responded metaphorically: "Tell that fox . . ." (Luke 13:32). The use of this word evidently refers to Herod's deceptive character.

Bread and wine are the metaphors used for the Lord's Supper. In June 2005 my wife and I went to Hawaii. One of the sites we visited was Pearl Harbor. On December 7, 1941, the Japanese bombed the Hawaiian naval fleet, sinking huge ships carrying multitudes of naval personnel to a watery grave. I could still see the presence of oil on the bosom of the water as I stood on the platform of the memorial, which was built over a sunken ship. There was great solemnity as the visitors walked across the memorial and went into the sanctuary that housed a white marble wall on which were engraved the names of all the persons who gave their lives so that America might remain free. Relatives of those who lay beneath the memorial visited this same place and wept uncontrollably as they remembered the life of a loved one given on behalf of their freedom.

I know a man who had a heart transplant. One of the first things he did after the operation was to express appreciation to the family of the donor for the gift of life and to request a picture of the donor so that he would always live with the donor's picture in the picture frame of his mind.

When believers come to the Lord's Supper table, they come with the picture of the divine donor hanging on a cross in the picture frame of their mind, and they adore the Lord who died so that they might live. No one took the Lord's life; he laid it down as a ransom for many (Mark 10:45). Believers are enveloped in an atmosphere of worship and reverence.

Jesus sent the disciples forth like wayward, defenseless, helpless sheep who would be surrounded by a ravenous pack of wolves. He wanted to teach them that their only defense was the sender—"I send you forth" (Matt 10:16). Jesus admonished them to be wise like serpents. Their wisdom must be exemplified by their constant trust in the sender. In addition to being wise like serpents, they must also be harmless as doves. Doves are gentle. Noah sent out a dove three times in order to ascertain whether the floodwaters had receded enough for him and his family to leave the ark, receiving his answer when the dove did not return after the third time. The Holy Spirit, in the form of a dove, rested on the shoulder of Jesus as he stood in the baptismal waters of the Jordan River. Doves are nonaggressive. They are not birds of prey.

It is interesting that our professional athletic teams, particularly professional football teams, are named after aggressive, not nonaggressive, birds. There are the Atlanta Falcons, the Philadelphia Eagles, and the Baltimore Ravens. No professional football team or amateur athletic team has ever named their team the Doves. But Jesus says, "Be . . . harmless as doves" (Matt 10:16). This metaphor suggests that believers do not have to fight their battle because the battle is the Lord's and not their own (cp. 2 Chron 20:15). As the Lord built a hedge around Job, prepared a table for David in the presence of his enemies, sent a militant angel to Jerusalem to protect King Hezekiah and his forces, and resurrected Jesus from the tomb on Sunday morning while it was yet dark, so the Lord protects the saints in their dovelike state. Saints are under the divine, protective custody of the Lord.

Metaphors are pictures. I have been in old church edifices with beautiful stained-glass windows. The windows from outside of the building do not yield their most impressive aesthetic value. Sometimes they look gray and dreary. But on the inside of the building when the light penetrates the glass, all of the colors are vividly displayed, and the stories behind the pictures are silently told. There is a nativity scene; obviously it is depicting the birth of the Christ child. There is a temple scene in which the twelve-year old Jesus is dialoguing with teachers. There is a baptismal scene where one man is baptizing another, a dove is sitting on the baptismal candidate's shoulder, and a cloud opens up as if someone is speaking, apparently referring to the baptism of Jesus the Son of God. There are three crosses on a hill, and the cross in the middle holds One who looks confident although He has been condemned, pointing to the crucifixion of Jesus. Eleven men are looking up into the atmosphere as they watch a man on a cloud ascend into the heights of heaven, certainly speaking of the ascension of Christ. These silent pictures tell the story of the earthly pilgrimage of Christ. There are some things that are too deep for words.

Biblical characters must be talked about so that the hearers see them as metaphors for their lives. The apostle Peter must be related so vividly that he comes out of the biblical picture frame and walks down the aisle of the sanctuary, conversing with the hearers about the Lord who gives failing believers another chance. Ruth must be communicated so movingly that she speaks through the corridor of time to twenty-first-century believers that God will remove the burden of a curse and grant a blessing that defies logic. Daniel must be articulated so cogently that he addresses today's believers about the significance of praying before the crisis, during the crisis, and after the crisis. The little lad whose two fish and five loaves served as the medium for a miracle must be illustrated so clearly that Christians lay hold to the truth: the Lord will use what you make available for Him. Some things are too deep for words.

Two Magnificent Metaphors

Two magnificent metaphors in this book buttress doctrinal preaching. They are the *exegetical escort* and the *doxological dancer*. The rationale for explaining and expounding on doctrinal preaching metaphorically is expressed in the metaphors of the escort and the dancer. *The function of the exegetical escort is to embrace the text of Scripture in order to usher the hearer into the presence of God for the purpose of transformation.* Preachers of Christian doctrine must draw out of the Bible what is in the Bible without projecting their own presuppositions and interests on the text. The authorial intention must be gleaned because a text can never mean today what it never meant when it was written. This is the work of exegesis. After embracing what the text meant when it was written, the exegetical escort ushers the hearers into the presence of God after showing them how the text applies to their lives and what response they need to make to the dictates of the text, then leaves them in the throne room of God's presence awaiting the transformation that only God can perform. There is no pressure for the exegetical escort to change anyone. The word of God goes out and does not return void; rather, it accomplishes the purpose for which it was sent (Isa 55:11). Sometimes the transformation is immediate, and sometimes it is like a time-released capsule of medicine; but the Word of God carries within its bosom the power to transform. How liberating it is to know that the doctrinal preacher is responsible for communication and not transformation!

The function of the doxological dancer is to communicate the doctrinal message of the Bible with accuracy and ardor so that the exuberant hearer exults in the exalting of God. The preacher of Christian doctrine is primarily a worshipper. Preaching is an act of worship. It is a gift, an offering of a sweet aroma up to the presence of God for the praise and glory of God. Thus, the Greek word for *doxology* means "praise" or "glory." The doctrinal preacher draws from the Bible its core teachings and communicates those with accuracy. In the words of the apostle Paul, the Word of God is to be "rightly divided" or "cut straight" (2 Tim 2:15). The Bible, being the Word of God, is truthful; however, it must be preached and taught not only with accuracy but also with ardor and enthusiasm. Our word *enthusiasm* comes from two Greek words, *en* and *theos*, meaning "in God." The proclaimer of Christian doctrine must proclaim the teachings of Scripture enthusiastically and exuberantly because both the proclamation and the proclaimer are in God. It is a sin to make the good news of the gospel "boring news" from the pulpit and classroom. Doctrinal preaching that is both accurate in its textual interpretation and ardent in its proclamation influences and motivates the hearers to be exuberant in their hearing of the message and to exult or rejoice in God during the preaching event while they are exalting God in the worship service.

How does one talk about the ineffable and unknowable God without using metaphors, the language of accommodation? Preachers must take metaphorical snapshots of the image of God. The Bible offers many metaphors of God draped in anthropomorphic language. Among them are a shield to protect, a rock that is stable, a warrior to deliver, a consuming fire to destroy, an eagle to transport, and a father to provide. Even with the use of metaphorical language, the preacher cannot say everything about God, for God will not be controlled by an image.

Dynamic Dance Steps for Doctrinal Preaching

While I was teaching a course on "Preaching in the African American Tradition" at Gordon-Conwell Theological Seminary, an Asian student made this confession: "My head is dancing, but my body won't move!"

Why is it when both preacher and people have their minds enlightened by the Word of God and their hearts touched by the Word of God, neither their voices nor their bodies give a resounding amen to the proclamation and acceptance of that word? "Let the 'amen' sound from His people again; gladly forever adore Him," says Joachim Neander in his hymn rendition, "Praise to the Lord, the Almighty."[11] Why is it that Romans 7 is more often quoted than Romans 8? Where is the victory of Romans 8 in our preaching?

Darrell Evans, in his song "Fields of Grace," has captured the celebrative mind-set of the preacher and people who worship God in spirit and in truth:

> There's a place that I love to run and play
> There's a place that I sing new songs of praise;
> There's a place that I lose myself within
> There's a place that I find myself again;
> There's a place where religion finally dies
> There's a place that I lose my selfish pride;
> I love my Father, my Father sings over me;
> Dancin' with my Father in the fields of grace,
> Dancin' with my Father in fields of grace[12]

11 "Praise to the Lord, the Almighty," words by Joachim Neander, "Lobe den Herren," 1665.
12 Darrell Evans, "Fields of Grace," copyright 2002 by Integrity's Hosanna! Music. Permission granted.

DOCTRINE *That* DANCES

To Dance or Not to Dance in Doctrinal Preaching

A choreographed dance is one in which the dancer has been given form, position, and musical timing; but the Spirit can instantaneously give unrehearsed steps that find rhythm with the choreographed, established steps. In Philippians 1:19 (NIV), the Greek word for "choreography" is *epichoregias:* "For I know that through your prayers and the help given by the Spirit of Jesus Christ, what has happened to me will turn out for my deliverance." The Holy Spirit is the choreographer who arranged for Paul to go to Rome to be a witness. Since the Holy Spirit knows what He is going to do, why prepare to dance? Why not yield to the movement of the ministry of the Spirit!

In the ministry of liturgical dancing, the liturgical dancer rehearses dance steps for the Sunday morning worship service and yet is willing to yield spontaneously to the Holy Spirit's deletion or addition of dance steps. The most important thing is the message; it must not change.

One of the big differences between liturgical dancing and secular dancing is that in the liturgical dance the emphasis is on the movement from the waist up, and in secular dancing the emphasis is on the movement from the waist down. The story is told basically from the heart up in the liturgical dance! Doctrinal preaching emphasizes the why of the dance rather than the how of the dance. It must be what is coming from the heart and spirit rather than what is happening with the feet. The facial expression and gesture should also indicate whether the dance and sermon are celebratory. The dancer and preacher must take people on a journey with them. The body movement must match the message of the song and the sermon. The message and the medium must be inextricably linked together.

There is a place for exuberance when people respond and for modification when people do not respond. If people choose not to respond, the liturgical dancer and preacher can't give God anything less than excellence. They are linked up as ministers to people from God. They cannot be conditioned by the moods and temperaments of the people because congregational moods and temperaments vacillate and fluctuate. Spirit must be chosen over soil and God's glory over human geography. Pausing is a big part of dancing and preaching. The body has to punctuate the lyrics and the mood of the biblical text. The dancer must know the words of the song, and the preacher must internalize the words of the sermon. Without knowing the material, both dancer and preacher become a sounding brass and a tinkling cymbal.

The Preacher as Dance Instructor

The minister who preaches sound Christian doctrine is uniquely gifted to be both exegetical escort who adheres to the written text of Scripture and doxological dancer who delivers the sermon in a passionate manner according to the tune of the Spirit.

On the evening of the birth of the Christ child, the shepherds heard the *text* of the angelic message: "Do not be afraid. I bring you good news of great joy that will be for all the people. Today in the town of David a Savior has been born to you; he is Christ the Lord. This will be a sign to you: you will find a baby wrapped in cloths and lying in a manger" (Luke 2:10–12 NIV). But the shepherds did not leave for Bethlehem until they heard the *tune* that accompanied the *text*: "Suddenly a great company of the heavenly host appeared with the angel, praising God and saying, 'Glory to God in the highest, and on earth peace to men on whom his favor rests'" (Luke 2:13–14 NIV). The preacher who preaches doctrine that dances must keep the authoritative *text* of Scripture and the arresting *tune* of style in tension throughout the preaching moment.

African American Dance Steps
for Doctrinal Preaching

Once I was asked by a publishing company editor to write a book demonstrating how blacks preach with passion so that whites could emulate passionate preaching by learning the steps. Harry Emerson Fosdick referred to Edmund Holt Linn, who had studied and analyzed his preaching methodology so well, and admitted, "I am simply stunned by the endless and meticulous labor . . . expended on everything I ever did or said. . . . You know much more about me than I know about myself. Again and again I gasped, as I read, recognizing in me something you had dug up—a long-forgotten incident or idea."[13] Many have the experience of preaching without necessarily understanding their own preaching process; consequently, they cannot articulate the etymology, evolution, and development of their homiletical methodology. I heard a taped interview of the renowned preacher Dr. Gardner C. Taylor, commenting about his college president, who made a statement that was rather puzzling to him: "It is better to fail with a plan than to succeed without one."[14] Years later Taylor admitted to gaining some understanding of what his college president meant. If you fail with a plan, you know what to do. If you succeed without one, you don't know how you succeeded in the first place. Although some things cannot be learned in a book and must be experienced, preaching can be enhanced not by imitation but by association and assimilation of other preaching traditions and homiletical art forms.

David Buttrick, former professor of homiletics at Vanderbilt Divinity School, stated in the appendix of his book *Homiletic*, "I have been influenced by the Black homiletic tradition. All things considered, it is probable that the finest preaching in America today is Black."[15] Thomas Long, while serving as professor of homiletics at the Princeton Theological Seminary, challenged the title "Dean of Black Preaching," a title given to Dr. Gardner C. Taylor, and contended that Dr. Taylor was the "Dean of all preaching in America."[16] The black preaching tradition gave birth to a sequential homileti-

13 Edmund Holt Linn, *Preaching as Counseling* (Valley Forge: Judson, 1966), 5.
14 Great Preachers Series, Series 1, featuring Dr. Gardner C. Taylor, produced by Odyssey Productions, Ltd., distributed 1997 by Vision Video, Worcester, PA.
15 David Buttrick, *Homiletic* (Philadelphia: Fortress, 1987), 469.
16 Ibid., 82.

cal structure that has been implemented by black preachers from generation to generation. It is a paradigmatic dictum for biblical preaching today that can be translated into preaching delivery steps. This dictum consists of six movements. These steps were taken from the United Kingdom tradition and adapted for use in the African American preaching tradition. Dr. James Stalker, during a lecture titled "The Preacher as Man of the Word," made these comments:

> An esteemed friend, the Rev. John McMillan of Ullapool, some years ago repeated to me the follow-ing rhyme on the method of constructing a sermon, and although I have never succeeded in coming up to its standard, it has often floated before me with advantage in the hours of composition:

> > Begin low;
> > Proceed slow;
> > Rise higher;
> > Take fire;
> > When most impressed
> > Be self-possessed;
> > To Spirit wed form
> > Sit down in a storm.[17]

These represent the sermonic dance steps for doctrinal preaching. The preacher, as an exegetical escort and doxological dancer, pro-gressively executes these dance steps in the preaching event.

Step One: Identification—"Start Low"

A good prechoreographic practice when dancing is always to warm up. This could be the introduction of the sermon or the preparation for the sermon. This is what gets the body, mind, and spirit together so that injury is avoided. One must medi-tatively stretch. I challenge my students to read their preaching

17 Cited by Edgar DeWitt Jones, *The Royalty of the Pulpit* (New York: Harper & Brothers, 1951), 183.

41

passage fifty times before they begin to research its implications for the hearers. In this way they expose all of their senses to the text, and the encounter of the senses with the text will be felt and seen through a delivery that is imbued with authority and humility. Preaching that dances starts low and begins where the people are.

Ezekiel spent seven days sitting with the Jewish exiles without opening his mouth (Ezek 3:15). After receiving a message he went to speak to the captives (11:13). Jesus sat by a well in Sychar and met the Samaritan woman where she was. Upon the completion of His talk to her, she became a missionary to the men of her city (John 4:39). Jesus used the same approach in speaking His parables. The effective preacher often starts in the world of the Bible and brings its message up to the modern world. God meets us where we are and takes us where He wants us to go.

Step Two: Clarification—"Go Slow"

If the praise dancer starts out too rapidly, the accelerated pace is harder to sustain and the message will be truncated. The listener will tend to give up on the message. As the listener becomes more comfortable, the preacher can increase the intensity. Jesus taught the twelve disciples in a period of three years. He said, "I have much more to say to you, more than you can now bear" (John 16:12 NIV). Fred Craddock, celebrated homiletician, advises the student preacher to write the conclusion of the sermon before the introduction is written because one cannot introduce what one does not have. When preachers have carefully and artfully constructed their sermons so that nothing is superfluous within the sermon, they are able to be deliberate in their delivery because they go forth knowing where they are going.

Step Three: Intensification—"Rise"

Biblical preaching rises to the occasion because it is Spirit directed and not *human centered*. It slowly rises toward a crescendo, handling the text in the power of the Spirit. The sermon must have movement. It must press its way toward a goal—exalting God through Christ, aware of Christ's promise: "I, when I am lifted up from the earth, will draw all men to myself" (John 12:32 NIV). Like an airplane, the sermon must leave the runway and take flight. Preachers need not fear the heights of emotion stirred by what is absorbed. There is always higher ground to be gained in the preaching moment.

Step Four: Application—"Strike Fire"

This is the place of energy, culmination, and power. The preacher wants the people to experience the meaning, the purpose, and the message. No text should ever be used to mean today what it never meant when it was written. Two weaknesses in preaching are in the areas of meaning and application. Relevant preaching requires that the written revelation be neither ignored nor misapplied. Jeremiah had the process correctly. The word of God was in his heart like fire shut up in his bones (Jer 20:9). The fire of his passion ignited his preaching.

Step Five: Recapitulation—"Retire"

In retiring is the "coming-down step"—the preacher is trusting God to affect the hearer. Retiring is concluding or summing up the message. The jazz musician said, "I'm like a minister giving his sermon. He will state his theme; he'll improvise variations on that theme; take it to a high point; and then he'll make his closing statement. I'm doing the same thing at the piano."[18]

Step Six: Motivation—"Sit Down in a Storm"

There is a "cool down" period after the dance in which the preacher eventually sits down in a storm. People are emotionally "still up" when the preacher "sits down." The message has been

18 Kirk Byron Jones, *The Jazz of Preaching* (Nashville: Abingdon, 2004), 35–36.

given and the people are worshipping. The people take the message home and live with it. They take home that "aha moment" where they understand something in their own lives because of what the preacher has said. So when the preacher sits down, the people should be getting up! They have to get up and do the work of ministry. They have to pick up the dance. If the preacher has taught them the dance, then they must get up and dance and tell the story to someone else.

Peter Taylor Forsyth defines preaching as "the organized Hallelujah of an ordered community."[19] He means that preachers preach so that the congregation will preach. The preacher dances so that the congregation will dance. The preachers should want their preaching to dance so that the hearers will dance in response. When the preacher finishes the sermon, the preacher should let it be. The Spirit is using the sermon before and after the benediction. Let it be, and let it live. It has its own life.

Lionel Hampton demonstrates "sitting down in a storm." He flays away first in the vibes, then on piano, using just two fingers like vibraphone mallets, then switches to a frantic, stick-tossing session on drums, and then climaxes the whole affair by jumping up onto a tom-tom and dancing wildly on top of it. Lionel must go down in history as one of the most inspiring and the most perspiring jazz musicians of all time.

A sermon starts like music with conflict, and then it gets worse through complication—things get worse before they get better. There is a decisive turnaround, a liberating moment through the preaching of the gospel. Like the big band sound, the preacher wraps it up and comes to a big crescendo. The people want an encore! The preacher sits down while the congregation thirsts for more.

19 Peter Taylor Forsyth, *Positive Preaching and the Modern Mind* (New York: Armstrong, 1901), 64.

Chapter Three

LORD OF THE DANCE AND THE ESCORT

*D*octrinal understanding prepares the preacher for preaching. Its task is to continually pass the baton to preaching. Doctrine must be preached; it is not an ivory tower engagement of a scholar divorced from an ongoing involvement with the congregation. Doctrine that cannot be preached is not real doctrine at all. It must be preachable!

Helmut Thielicke, German theologian-preacher, believed that the study of doctrine was never to be the sole endeavor of the scholar; rather, both the church and the pulpit scholar must be knowledgeable of the doctrine of Scripture. This is why Thielicke chose to deliver a weeklong seminar on the Apostles' Creed at St. Michael's Church in Hamburg, Germany. This church had a seating capacity of over three thousand, and he filled the building for each presentation. He discovered that people had inquiring minds and wanted to know about the profound and prodigious claims of Scripture: death, the resurrection of the body, eternal life, and God. During this weeklong seminar, he attempted to display the totality of the Christian faith as viewed through the lens of the Apostles' Creed.

Preachers must not evade the task of doctrinal preaching because of the hard and disciplined work that goes into it. The late Sandy F. Ray, the noted African American pulpiteer and pastor of Cornerstone Baptist Church in Brooklyn, New York, graphically depicted the work of the doctrinal preacher. He compared this type of preaching to a mountain that had to be dismantled, broken into small portions, loaded on the truck, and carried to the church for each member to consume in bite-size pieces. The pastor is a resident theologian who goes into the study and wrestles with the profound mysteries of doctrine and theology, comprehends those truths, and makes the complex information comprehensible when mounting the pulpit on Sunday morning.

The doctrinal preacher is to be rooted in doctrine but not buried in it. People who listen to our preaching have at least three basic questions: *what*, which focuses on information; *so what*, which deals with contemporization; and *now what*, which relates to motivation. Those who would preach the great doctrines of the Bible must be true to the revelation of God and aware of a relevant word for the people. Doctrinal preachers are not only exegetes of the text but of the congregation as well. They transition from the "Word that was" to the "Word that is." During the sermon the ancient text and the contemporary listener are in constant dialogue with each other. In the language of Anglican pastor-scholar John R. W. Stott, the doctrinal preacher stands between two worlds: "A true sermon bridges the gulf between the biblical and modern worlds, and must be equally earthed in both."[1] This is necessary so that the figures within the picture frame of Scripture can come out during the sermon, walk down the aisles of the church, and have a conversation with the contemporary worshippers. This is why Ray Steadman, renowned expositor frequently in conferences across America, denies that the New Testament is twenty centuries old, instead contending that the New Testament is one century old repeated for twenty centuries. This was also the conviction of James A. Sanders, a professor of canonical hermeneutics, who helped us to see that the biblical characters did not primarily serve as models for morality but as mirrors for identity. He said, "Most biblical texts must be read, not by looking in them for models for morality, but by looking in them for mirrors for identity."[2] Furthermore, Sanders comments: "And this may be done by reading the story not as though it were of events way back

---

1 John R. W. Stott, *Between Two Worlds* (Grand Rapids: Eerdmans, 1982), 10.
2 James A. Sanders, "Hermeneutics," in *The Interpreter's Dictionary of the Bible*, supplementary volume (Nashville: Abingdon Press, 1976), 406.

there about ancient folk but by reading it dynamically, identifying with those who provide us the best mirrors of our identity."[3] Doctrinal preaching, even at its best, does not answer all the questions about the incarnation, the Trinity, and other primary doctrines; but it helps contemporary listeners see their faces alongside the faces of characters in the biblical photo album. Many Christians criticize and laugh at Simon Peter because they recognize many of his traits in themselves: we are like Peter. We are like Abraham, who laughed at the promise of God. We are like the woman at the well, who could not be satisfied until she had her thirst quenched by the living water. Consequently, doctrinal preaching does not motivate the hearer to be like the biblical character; they are already. The challenge of doctrinal preaching is for the believer to be transformed into the image of Christ.

The Burdensome Joy

Dr. James Earl Massey, former dean of the School of Theology of Anderson University, delivered the William E. Conger Jr. Lectures on Preaching at Beeson Divinity School in 1995. In lectures titled "The Burdensome Joy of Preaching,"[4] Massey argued for the paradox of burden and joy in preaching. Gardner C. Taylor, former pastor of the Concord Baptist Church of Christ in Brooklyn, New York, sees preaching as the "sweet torture of Sunday morning."[5] This phrase is reminiscent of Shakespeare's famed line, "Parting is such sweet sorrow."[6] Taylor sees preaching as an investment in sorrow, pain, and struggle during the week of preparation; but on Sunday morning it transitions to sweetness. Both Taylor and Massey have their hands on the pulsating heartbeat of preaching Bible doctrine. It is a burden, an exercise in pain and

3 James A. Sanders, *God Has a Story Too* (Philadelphia: Fortress, 1979), 22.
4 The series of lectures was published by Abingdon Press under the same title.
5 James Earl Massey, "The Burdensome Joy of Preaching," *Leadership Magazine*, Summer 1981.
6 William Shakespeare, *Romeo and Juliet* 2.2, 198–200.

sorrow that finally yields to joy. The preacher, like the Israelites in Nehemiah's and Ezra's day, responds to the revelation in reading God's Word with tears and sorrow and yet recognizes that that same Word offers sweetness and joy. Nehemiah tells the people to eat the fat and drink the sweet wine and declare that the joy of the Lord is their strength (Neh 8:10). Those who would preach Bible doctrine must assume the posture of Naomi, who went out full and returned to Bethlehem empty. Preachers must leave the study full and preach themselves empty in the pulpit. It is to be likened to the image of pregnancy: the preacher is impregnated with the Word during the week and delivers the offspring in the form of the sermon on Sunday.

We are not to handle the Bible as if it were just one more book merely to be studied and analyzed. The Bible provides more than information. In the purview of systematician Karl Barth, the gospel (the spoken Word) and the Bible (the written Word) serve as vehicles to transport the hearers to Jesus Christ (the revealed Word). Information alone will never change the hearts of human beings. That is why preaching to the mind alone is not enough.

The strange thing about Scripture is that it does not aim to make us understand doctrine in a systematic way. God wants to prevent humans from merely getting hold of doctrines; God wants the truth of the doctrines to get hold of humans. The apostle Paul expends nearly eleven chapters plumbing the depths of the profound doctrines in the book of Romans: justification, sanctification, glorification, creation, pneumatology, Christology, and anthropology, along with several other doctrinal truths. It is as if he pauses at the end of the eleventh chapter to sing a song of praise to God for His mighty acts and deeds in perfecting salvation's plan for humans. Paul sings this song after bombarding the minds of his hearers with the mysterious workings of the Almighty God: "O the depth of the riches both of the wisdom and knowledge of God! how unsearchable are his judgments, and his ways past finding out!" (Rom 11:33).

Lord of the Dance and the Escort

Doctrinal Bifocality

Doctrinal preaching has a set of bifocal lenses: it has a vertical orientation in which it envisions the revelation of the Word of God, and it looks horizontally and sees the need for relevance in presenting that Word to human beings. In his poem "The Windows," George Herbert, an English poet, captures the importance of discovering doctrine in life and life in doctrine:

> Doctrine and life, colours and light in one;
> When they combine and mingle, bring
> A strong regard and aw: but speech alone
> Doth vanish like a flaming thing,
> And in the eare, not conscience ring.[7]

So there must be a coinherence of doctrine and life. Herbert H. Farmer reinforces the need for doctrinal bifocality in his 1941 Warrick Lectures: "One thing is clear—our preaching has got to be strongly doctrinal, not in the manner of the theological lecture room, but in such, wise that doctrine and life are seen to be inseparably bound up together. It has got to teach the Christian interpretation of life in all its fullness."[8] Systematic theologian Paul Tillich reinforced this idea of doctrinal bifocality in his contention that doctrine "is the statement of the truth of the Christian message and the interpretation of this truth for every new generation."[9] Doctrinal preachers are also bifocal, having their head pointed toward the heavens and their feet on the ground. Doctrinal preaching is incarnational; it has a personal touch that is empowered by the Spirit of God. It is God's Word from the past, addressing our world in the present so that we may live forever with Him in the future. In a conversation during the

7 George Herbert, *The Poetical Works of George Herbert* (New York: D. Appleton and Co., 1857), 83. Submitted by Dean Timothy George, Beeson Divinity School, Birmingham, Alabama, quoting one of his favorite poets.
8 Herbert H. Farmer, *The Servant of the Word* (London: Religious Book Club, 1941), 143.
9 Paul Tillich, *Systematic Theology* (Chicago: University of Chicago Press, 1951), 1:3.

49

March 6, 1991 E. Y. Mullins Lectures on Preaching at the Southern Baptist Theological Seminary, Fred Craddock told of a preacher who took a trip and brought back a slide presentation to share with the congregation. Preachers cannot bring back the entire trip and experience; they can only share what has been learned and experienced and invite the hearers to experience the same.[10] It is because of what God has done in Christ that we are able to say, "By the grace of God I am what I am" (1 Cor 15:10).

Helmut Thielicke believed in the efficacious work of the gospel as it relates to human frailty. He offered this pertinent and powerfully moving personal experience:

> After an air attack I was helping with the cleanup operations and was standing at the edge of a huge crater opened up by an aerial bomb. A woman came up to me—she was the wife of the officer who had been killed. . . . She then showed me her husband's cap and said, "This is all that was left of him. Only last Thursday, I was with him, attending your lecture. And now I want to thank you for preparing him for his death." Then she quietly shook my hand.[11]

The minister of the gospel is called to specialize in living and not just to be astute in doctrine. Ultimately doctrinal preaching seeks to prepare people for eternity by ushering them into the presence of God.

Doctrinal Hybridity: Head and Heart

In a conversation with British theologian Alister McGrath, former archbishop of Canterbury Donald Loggan remarked, "The

---

10 Conversation with Dr. Fred B. Craddock, March 6, 1991, during the E. Y. Mullins Lectures on Preaching at Southern Baptist Theological Seminary, Louisville, KY.

11 Helmut Thielicke, *Man in God's World*, trans. John W. Doberstein (New York: Harper & Row, 1963), 10.

journey from head to heart is one of the longest and most difficult we know."[12] Sometimes, the doctrinal preacher will begin with the head and move to the heart; other times the direction will be reversed. Regardless of the starting point, the end result must always be the same: the inclusivity of both. We are experiencing a kind of "dumbing down," a dismantling of the triumph of the mind, and people are turning to easy "believism" and naïve quick fixes to life's problems. The mind is certainly not enough, but neither is the heart. Jesus said that we are to love God with all our hearts and minds (Matt 22:37).

At times we preach to a *beheaded* people. They enter into the sanctuary with hearts alone. Their chief interest is inspiration. They want to feel better. They desire a therapy session. They want to be touched and moved. However, they have little interest in the matters of the mind. At other times, though, we preach to a *big-headed* people who have no heart for the inspiration of the Word. They want to know more; they want the gray matter of their brains to be expanded. Their interest is in scholarship. Feeling is not on their list of expectations. It is not an either/or proposition; it is a both/and reality. If God is to be worshipped in spirit and in truth, then preaching Bible doctrine must touch the realm of the spirit (heart) and the realm of truth (mind). Upon becoming a Christian, one is not expected to check in or drop off one's intelligence in the vestibule. By the same token, though, Christians are not to deposit their spirit in the narthex. The whole person is to enter the sanctuary to be engaged by the whole counsel of God.

As preachers, we are called into a relationship with the Word. The Hebrew word for knowledge is *yadah*. It is also used relationally for lovemaking: "Now Adam knew Eve his wife, and she conceived and bore Cain" (Gen 4:1 ESV). The Greek word for knowledge is *gnosis*. "And Mary said to the angel, 'How will this be, seeing I know not a man?'" (Luke 1:34 ESV). These two words for

12 Timothy George and Alister McGrath, eds., *For All the Saints* (Louisville: Westminster John Knox, 2003), 11–12.

"knowing" in both the Hebrew and Greek traditions involve rela-tionships. The Hebrew term, *lav*, the word for *heart*, does not exclude but rather includes the rational sector of human existence. It is the whole center of the person. For Elie Wiesel, the study of the Torah was likened to crawling in the cranium of *Yahweh*. This was an exercise in cognitive knowing which was intended to result in an affective response that called one to obedience in behavior. There is no antithesis between an informed head and an inspired heart. The one who would preach doctrinally must simultaneously be operating on both tracks of the head and the heart.

The ancient prophet Jeremiah experienced divine interpene-tration in both areas. He had determined to turn in his prophetic license to God and had made up his mind not to preach in the name of *Yahweh* anymore. But God's Word, which he knew well, was not only in his mind but also in his heart. It was like fire shut up in his bones, and he eventually had to rescind his plan for early retirement from the ministry (Jer 20:9).

What can the church say in its proclamation that no one else can say? What is unique about the message of doctrinal preach-ing? Since those who preach doctrine are not ventriloquists, what do they proclaim that is not only engaging and transformative but unique? Doctrinal preaching is about the proclamation of a fact; Jesus Christ is that fact. We must reclaim the mantle of doctrine in our preaching. It is a birthright that was given to us by our Lord. He said, ". . . teaching them to observe all that I have com-manded you" (Matt 28:19 ESV).

Doctrinal preaching happens from the overflow of one's engagement with the Scriptures, from ministers who not only read the text, but the text has also read them. Doctrinal preaching is a marriage of the truth of biblical doctrine with the tune of the sermonic presentation. It is belief exemplified in behavior, and it is substance welded with style. Preaching has wings that fly, but it also has an anchor that holds. It turns the ink of the written word into the blood of authentic Christian living. Doctrinal preaching is a road map that leads to Christ. It initiates the hearer into faith through proclamation; it instructs the hearer in the faith through teaching; and it inspires the hearer to keep the faith through therapy. All of this serves to usher people into the presence of God for the purpose of transformation.

Reformer Martin Luther made the clarion call to his colleagues *ad fontes*—to the sources. Originally it was a call to reclaim the heritage of Greek and Roman antiquity. Luther adopted this Renaissance phrase and baptized it. He was not calling for a cultural reformation; rather, he was attempting to move the church to a spiritual and biblical reformation. For him it meant going back to the fundamentals of Christianity: *sola gratia, sola fides, solus Christus,* and *sola scriptura* (grace, faith, Christ, and Scripture only). Dr. James Cox, professor of preaching at the Southern Baptist Theological Seminary, sees doctrine as the iron rods that hold the concrete of preaching together.[13] Motorists drive over the highway every day with little or no thought of the iron rods that lie beneath the concrete surface. These rods provide connection and enable the concrete to remain intact and withstand the constant pressure of the ongoing traffic.

A key to an effective pastoral ministry is serving the congregation a regular diet that nourishes both the mind and the heart. As scaffolding helps to form the building under construction, doctrine informs the sermon. The scaffold is retired after the building is completed. Similarly, the real object of doctrine is not the doctrine itself; rather, the doctrine points beyond itself to the person of Christ. Doctrine is like a road sign that points to a destination. Consequently, if the doctrine is preached without focusing upon the person of Christ, then it is lifeless and insipid. Martin Luther's analogy of the swaddling clothes that contained the Christ to the Scriptures that enfold Jesus, the self-revelation of God, is picturesquely poignant.

---

13 Conversation with Dr. James Cox, February 23, 1991.

Today biblical illiteracy abounds. Preachers who are serious about the whole counsel of God cannot depend upon the congregation's comprehensive knowledge of the Bible. There was a time when preachers could give a portion of a biblical narrative and assume that the hearer could make the connection. They would say in passing, "You know the story." The preacher no longer has that luxury. Church members do not necessarily know the story; we have to tell the story. There was a time when pastors could depend upon evangelists to do doctrinal preaching in their stead. For a pastor to make this assumption today would be an abdication of the pastor's role as resident theologian. In today's society young people in particular are looking for something that is certain and trustworthy. They want facts but not facts divorced from experience. Harry Emerson Fosdick said, "The rebirth of Christian emphasis on doctrine is not first of all the Christian's doing; our enemies have forced it on us."[14] Seekers in this generation are looking for the reality of experience and the experience of reality. Jesus' words reverberate through the corridors of twenty centuries: "And ye shall know the truth, and the truth shall make you free" (John 8:32). He offers an experience gained by truth.

Truth is often experienced before it is comprehended. In a commentary on John 9, Helmut Thielicke, the German preacher, reminds us that the blind man had an experience with Jesus without initially comprehending the encounter. When asked about Jesus, he responded, "Whether he is a sinner I do not know. One thing I do know, that though I was blind, now I see" (John 9:25 ESV). There is no question that the blind man had received his sight, but his understanding of who performed the miracle and how it took place was deficient. It was not until after he was excommunicated from the synagogue and visited by Jesus that his understanding caught up with his experience. Jesus asked him, "Do you believe

---

14 Harry Emerson Fosdick, "A Religion That Really Gets Us," in *What Is Vital in Religion* (New York: Harper & Brothers, 1900), 58.

in the Messiah?" He responded, "I would, if I knew who he was." Jesus said, "I am He." The man believed.

The Question of God

Doctrinal preaching's greatest interest is that God be presented clearly and accurately. Our task is articulated by Philip's request to Jesus: "Lord, show us the Father" (John 14:8 NIV). Those who come to hear us need to hear about more than international disasters, relational rifts, and painful predicaments. The greatest need that a human being has is to see God. For those who hear us, God is not only the answer but also the question.

There was a time, in the early years of my ministry, when people understood that whenever I made reference to God, I was talking about the God who created the heavens and the earth. Today, however, when preachers talk about God, they must clarify *which* God. The question behind all questions is the question of God. This is Helmut Thielicke's posture through his work *The Hidden Question of God*.[15] Fred Craddock, a well-respected homiletician, asserted that somewhere, lurking in the backwoods of a person's mind, is the God question. Augustine cried to God, "Thou hast formed us for Thyself, and our hearts are restless until they find rest in Thee."[16] Leo Tolstoy also believed that people who sin have a God-sized hole in them, a hole that only God can fill. Bryan Chapell, president of Covenant Theological Seminary in St. Louis, Missouri, suggested that a congregation is filled with holes like a piece of Swiss cheese, and that only the Word of God can fill the holes.[17] I would add that not only the Word of God but the God of the Word fills the holes.

15 Helmut Thielicke, *The Hidden Question of God*, trans. Geoffrey W. Bromiley (Grand Rapids: Eerdmans, 1979).
16 Augustine of Hippo, *Confessions*, trans. William Watts (Cambridge, MA: Harvard University Press, 1912), 1.
17 Bryan Chapell, E. Y. Mullins Lectures on Preaching at Southern Baptist Theological Seminary, Louisville, KY, March 6, 1996.

It is not enough for us to preach doctrine to people for the sole purpose of informing them about the attributes of God: God's holiness, justice, faithfulness, and love. People must do more than just know about God; they must know *God*. This is the sentiment of the apostle Paul who yearned to know God. In Philippians 3:10, he said, "That I may know him . . ." Paul knew a lot about God. He knew about His grace that changed him from the church's number one public enemy to the church's number one public defender. He knew about God's election, which called him, chose him, and placed him in the ministry in preexistent eternity. He knew about God's love, which was immeasurable. He knew about God's riches in Christ, which were unsearchable. He knew about God's gift through Christ, which was unspeakable. One would think that if anyone knew God, that person was Paul.

But Paul understood that the one who knows the most about God is also the one who recognizes how much of God there is to know. Rudolf Otto, in his book *The Idea of the Holy*, speaks of the *mysterium tremendum*—the tremendous mystery. People do not *get* God, although they are always seeking after Him. *God gets them.* Therefore it is important that preachers present the God of Bible doctrine and not some one-size-fits-all kind of God who can be made into the image and likeness of the likes and whims of humans. English theologian Alister McGrath articulately puts it this way: "My experience is that we need to *go deeper* rather than just *know more*."[18] J. I. Packer affirms this in his work *Knowing God*. The question that Christians must always ask is the question that centers on what God wants to do through us rather than what God can do for us. Too often preachers make the mistake of focusing on the hand of God— what God can do *for us*—rather than on the heart of God—what God wants to do *through us*.

18 Alister McGrath, "Loving God with Heart and Mind," in *For All the Saints*, ed. McGrath and George, 13.

Those who preach doctrinally present God in the light of all Scripture. The ultimate reason for preaching doctrine is that it gives a true picture of God. J. B. Phillips' book *Your God Is Too Small* displays various caricatures of God: the Grand Old Man, who is senile and allows disobedience to exist without accountability; the resident policeman, who enjoys using a billy club to punish His people; and the God in a Box, who always responds when His people have an emergency but has no relationship with them outside of the crisis. God is not a "theological bell hop" or an "ecclesiastical red cap."[19] God is sovereign and is to be served by His creation. Having a correct image of God supplies believers with a true picture of their position as Christians: God is *with us*, God is *for us*, and God is *in us* through the power of the Holy Spirit. From a trinitarian perspective, we believe in God the Father, through Jesus the Son, by the power of the Holy Spirit.

How does the One who is before creation and who will be after the consummation of time teach us Bible doctrine? How does the One who knows our thoughts "afar off" instruct us about the wonderful words of life? How does the One who needs no one to counsel Him tutor us in the fundamentals of biblical thought?

The Bible is God's teaching manual. He writes it backwards, knowing the end before the beginning even begins (Isa 46:10; Rev 13:8). The apostle Paul speaks to the Roman Christians about the purpose of Scripture. In his thought Scripture exists for our learning (Rom 15:4). Throughout the Scriptures, God, as the omniscient teacher of the universe, brings us into His classroom and uses the textbook of the inspired Word to teach Bible doctrine. The Bible is vivid and diverse in its doctrinal expression. Unfortunately, as preachers and teachers of doctrine, we often make the Scriptures a portrait of predictable sameness. The Bible is a tapestry composed of inextricable, intertwining, and intersecting strands of surprising, dramatic, and unpredictable events interwoven in the fabric of God's written revelation

19 J. B. Phillips, *Your God Is Too Small* (New York: MacMillan, 1963), iii.

to humankind. How then does God use this doctrinal manual composed of diverse literary genres to instruct believers in the ways of the Lord?

Warren W. Wiersbe, in his book *Index of Biblical Images*, acknowledges the proverb, "The great teacher is the one who turns our ears into eyes so that we can see the truth."[20] God uses visual aids in the Bible to teach doctrine. The Bible is God's picture book. God says what He sees so clearly that we can see what God says. Our prayer to God while we read His Word should be,

> Open my eyes, that I may see
> Glimpses of truth thou hast for me . . .
> Open my eyes, illumine me,
> Spirit divine.[21]

Throughout the Bible, an ensemble of literary eyewitnesses provides visual snapshots of doctrinal lessons that God wants to teach His people. As they take their places on the stage of biblical history, they are identified as prophets, priests, kings, queens, apostles, and historians. They have one common method for teaching doctrine: visual or illustrative language. This "picture book" called the Bible is designed to display the mighty acts of God from creation to the coronation, and ultimately the consummation. Interestingly, the fabric and texture of this "picture book" is interwoven with the strands of secular stories that are baptized for sacred use. These sacred images are subverted, turned on their heads, and used for the purpose of teaching "sacred lessons" through the lens of secularity. With God there is no sacred/secular dichotomy. "The earth is the Lord's, and the fullness thereof; the world, and they that dwell therein" (Ps 24:1). God takes what is plain and crowns it with splendor. God takes the mundane and bestows it with majesty. God takes what is raw and wraps it up in radiance. Is this not the miracle of the incarnation? "The Word

---

20 Warren W. Wiersbe, *Index of Biblical Images* (Grand Rapids: Baker, 2000), 9.
21 Clara H. Scott, "Open My Eyes, That I May See," 1895.

became flesh and dwelt among us, and we have seen his glory, glory as of the only Son from the Father, full of grace and truth" (John 1:14 ESV). Great spiritual lessons are to be discerned in the transformation of linguistic secularity and not apart from it.

God, the Master Artist, teaches doctrine in a dramatic manner. The Bible opens with the *creation*. "In the beginning God created the heavens and the earth"—*creatio ex nihilo*. He created it out of nothing because there was nothing available. He came from nowhere because there was nowhere to come from. He stood on nothing because there was nothing to stand upon. He took nothing and made something. He put the sun in the sky without an upright and put the nine planets in a merry-go-round system around the sun without causing a collision. He painted the sky blue without a stepladder or a paintbrush. He made the fluffy, floating, fleecy white clouds. He carpeted the earth with green grass. He scooped out valleys and piled up mountains and wrote the songs for the birds to sing. This is the linguistic fashion in which the African American preacher often describes the divine display of the creative power of God.

Not only is the *creation* dramatically depicted, the *incarnation* is as well: "In the beginning was the Word, and the Word was with God, and the Word was God. . . . And the Word became flesh and dwelt among us, and we have seen his glory, glory as of the only Son from the Father, full of grace and truth" (John 1:1,14 ESV). Sallie McFague in *Models of God* says that Jesus of Nazareth "is a paradigm of God's relationship to the world."[22] Theologian Edward Schillebeeckx portrays Jesus "as the only true face of God."[23] So we can translate John 1:14, "In the beginning was the *Story*, and the *Story* was with God, and the *Story* was God. And the *Story* was made flesh and dwelt among us." What could be more dramatic and picturesque than God coming out of God's self and

22 Sallie McFague, *Models of God: Theology for an Ecological, Nuclear Age* (Philadelphia: Fortress, 1987), 56.
23 Edward Schillebeeckx, *Jesus: An Experiment in Christology* (New York: Crossroad, 1991), 146.

becoming human without forfeiting deity? He caught the train of nature and rode it for nine months, getting off at a little town called Bethlehem. The angelic choir in rarified air announced the birth of the incarnate One.

The *crucifixion* is also dramatic in its description. Were you there when they crucified my Lord? This is the penetrating and sobering question posed by the great Negro spiritual "Were You There When They Crucified My Lord?" Jesus was not crucified between two candles; He was crucified between two thieves. Grace was operative at Calvary, for a thief made the transition from eternal gloom to eternal glory just before death.

Finally, the *coronation* is dramatic in its climactic revelation. In the book of Revelation, the Lord is both lamb and lion and is praised for providing redemption through His death. John lets us eavesdrop on this praise service: "Worthy are you to take the scroll and to open its seals, for you were slain, and by your blood you ransomed people for God from every tribe and language and people and nation, and you have made them a kingdom and priests to our God, and they shall reign on the earth" (Rev 5:9–10 ESV).

God uses *words* when teaching doctrine. The children of Israel gathered around the quaking, smoking mountain of Sinai and requested that the "speaking God" refrain from word usage and let Moses speak in His place.

God uses *songs* to teach doctrine. The Song of Deborah in Judges 5 established the truth that God is so sovereign that He can allow the enemies to inflict pain upon His people and then give His people power to overthrow them. The Song of Moses in Deuteronomy 32 challenged the Israelites to remember the graciousness of God in bringing them *out of* Egypt *into* the wilderness on their way to the promised land, and it taught future generations that God's purposes cannot be thwarted. The Song of Hannah exulted in God for His provision of her son Samuel and verbalized the truth that God is faithful. The Hebrew psalter captured the fiber and fabric of the various moods of human beings and focused on God who is both immanent within the sphere of the human predicament and yet transcendent over all human circumstances. The Magnificat of Mary in Luke 1 grappled with the mystery of her being chosen without merit but by grace and the incomprehensible act of the Son of God becoming her son through the Holy Spirit. The *Nunc Dimittis*, or the Song of Simeon in Luke 2, lyrically proclaimed the providence of God in divinely managing that kairotic moment for the Christ child to be born and for Simeon to announce that he was ready to take his exit from earth. The Benedictus of Zacharias in Luke 1 acknowledged that his silence was broken after nine months, and he resorted to praising God. God broke His silence after four hundred years and kept His Word concerning a forerunner to the Christ and the invincibility of the King whose kingdom shall overthrow all other kingdoms. The great Christological hymn of Philippians 2:5–11 in encapsulated form depicts the enthronement of Jesus, His incarnation and condescension on earth, His obedience to the Father and suffering on the behalf of His human creation, His substitutionary atonement through the ignominious death on the cross, and finally His burial, resurrection, ascension, and exaltation. Finally, the Song of Moses and the Lamb in Revelation 5 punctuates the veracity of what has always been known in heaven and has to be instructed to human beings on earth: God is great and marvelous in His actions, righteous and true in His works, holy in His nature, and worthy of glory and praise.

God uses *pictures* when preaching doctrine. A little girl was once asked, "Which do you like better, the radio or the television?" She replied, "The radio, because the pictures are clearer!" Concepts are often difficult to concretize and make plain for the mind's eye. God teaches doctrine by drawing clear pictures of providence and security. In Deuteronomy 32:9–12 (ESV), He speaks in a picture to illustrate these realities:

> But the LORD's portion is his people, Jacob his allotted heritage. He found him in a desert land, and

in the howling waste of the wilderness; he encircled him, he cared for him, he kept him as the apple of his eye. Like an eagle that stirs up its nest, that flutters over its young, spreading out its wings, catching them, bearing them on its pinions, the LORD alone guided him, no foreign god was with him.

Believers see a vivid picture of how much God providentially provides for them when they reflect on the innate propensity of the eagle to swoop down from the nest, catch her eaglets in their failed initial attempts to fly, and carry them back to the security of the nest.

God teaches doctrine through *biographical snapshots*. We see ourselves in biblical characters and recognize our pictures alongside theirs in the Bible's pictorial art gallery and thereby discern the doctrinal lessons God is teaching us through them. We learn from David that if we cover our sins we will not prosper. Sin has to be covered by the blood of the Lamb of God and not by us. Someone used to say, "For every New Testament doctrine there is an Old Testament picture." Paul said to Titus that our sins were wiped clean "after that the kindness and love of God our Saviour toward man appeared" (Titus 3:4). Titus 3:4 identifies the New Testament doctrine of kindness, and 2 Samuel 9:3 illustrates the Old Testament picture of kindness. Saul, his son Jonathan, and most of his family had been decimated by the Philistines. Because those Philistines were attempting to wipe out every descendant of Saul's house, Jonathan's young son Mephibosheth was immediately carried to safety by his nurse. In her haste to escape with his life, though, he was dropped and was crippled. After David established his kingdom and gained victory over his enemies, he remembered the friendship he had shared with Jonathan and the promise he had made to "show kindness" to Jonathan's family. He asked, "Is there yet any that is left of the house of Saul, that I may show him kindness for Jonathan's sake?" (2 Sam 9:1). David treated Mephibosheth with kindness not because he deserved it but because he was the son of Jonathan, David's friend. This is a clear picture of the kindness of God. We are recipients of God's grace and kindness because of what Jesus, the Son of God, has done for us and the relationship that we have with Him.

God also teaches doctrine throughout the book of Proverbs, but many fail to see that Proverbs is a doctrinal book. For example, the word *skillful* in the book of Proverbs speaks of the skillful management of one's life. God teaches us through the metaphorical language in Proverbs how to skillfully manage our lives. There are verses in the book of Proverbs that are saturated in doctrine. Proverbs 4:18 (NIV) notes that, "The path of the righteous is like the first gleam of dawn, shining ever brighter till the full light of day." This is an excellent text for preaching on the advent of the Lord Jesus Christ. It can also be used in conjunction with the three times the light gets brighter in the testimony of Paul's conversion experience. In Acts 9:3 (NIV), "Suddenly a *light* from heaven flashed around him"; in Acts 22:6 (NIV), "suddenly a *bright light* from heaven flashed around me"; and in Acts 26:13 (NIV) "*a light* from heaven *brighter than the sun* blazing around me." The doctrine in that verse is the path of the just. Life is a path, and there is a destination. The path of those who are justified is a path "from grace to grace" and "from glory to glory." Growing up in my small African American church, I used to hear the choir sing the Negro spiritual "We Are Climbing Jacob's Ladder." One of the lines that always intrigued me was, "Every round goes higher, higher." God has predestined the path of the just in order to bring them closer to Christ, who is the light of the world. Analogically, in the book of Ruth, God is teaching doctrine through a love story. God is not only getting a bride, He is also getting a harvest. This anticipated the day of Pentecost when God would receive His bride, for the church was birthed on that day. There is also a harvest, for approximately three thousand persons were saved.

God also teaches doctrine through *metaphors*. One of His most effective ways of addressing the concept of sin is by painting a picture. How is the concept of sin related in Scripture? It's related through word pictures and metaphors. The word for *sin* in both the Old and New Testament is taken from the sport of archery. It suggests that sin is like an archer "missing the mark." Thus, sin is any word, thought, or deed that fails to "hit the mark" of God's intention of perfection for our lives. No wonder the Scriptures adamantly pour contempt upon human pride with such denunciations as: "All we like sheep have gone astray" (Isa 53:6); "All have sinned, and come short of the glory of God" (Rom 3:23); and "There is none righteous, no, not one" (Rom 3:10).

The metaphor of clothing as a covering for sin runs throughout the Bible, beginning with the moment the Lord replaces the Edenic residents' pathetic fig leaves with leather skins. This provides us with a glimpse into the "double type" of redemption: the Lord's redemption deals with cleansing and with covering. The Lord killed an animal, and blood was shed. He took the skins of the animal and clothed Adam and Eve with them (Gen 3:21). This is suggestive of the reality of being cleansed by the blood and clothed by the righteousness of God. The "redemptive double-type" is also discerned in Isaiah 53:7, for the lamb is led to the slaughter for some blood and the sheep to the shearers for some wool. In Luke 15:22–23, the return of the prodigal son moves the father to have the fattened calf killed; blood is shed, and his son is covered with the father's robe. In the book of Revelation, John gloriously depicts the saints as they go "marching in" as those who have washed their robes (covering) and made them white in the blood of the lamb (cleansing). Believers are "dressed in His righteousness alone, faultless to stand before the throne."

The Lord teaches doctrine through *discipline*, and He disciplines those He loves. David learned this, for he confessed, "Before I was afflicted I went astray, but now I obey your word" (Ps 119:67). Jonah discovered this when God made reservations for him to spend three days in the belly of a divinely custom-made fish, and this motivated him to seek God in prayer. The Jews experienced this after their seventy years of Babylonian incarceration. They were sentenced for idolatry, released, and returned to their land.

Paul was afflicted with an agonizing, almost unbearable pain predicament he called a "thorn in the flesh," but he does not define it in medical terms like malaria or scoliosis. Psychologically, it undoubtedly baffled, befuddled, and bewildered him. Physiologically, it probably deformed and disfigured him, limiting him in mobility. But spiritually and theologically it served as the matrix out of which he matured in Christ. Paul lets us look through the keyhole of his encounter with the Lord and eavesdrop on the Lord's enabling words to him: "My grace is sufficient for thee: for my strength is made perfect in weakness" (2 Cor 12:9). Paul emerges from this encounter with a glowing testimony that rings through the corridor of time and has encouraged many saints in the hospitals, pastors in crisis-ridden congregations, spouses who were deserted, and missionaries who at times felt forsaken: "Therefore I take pleasure in infirmities, in reproaches, in necessities, in persecutions, in distresses for Christ's sake: for when I am weak, then am I strong" (2 Cor 12:10). Similarly, Charles Haddon Spurgeon used to say that "the promises of God never shine brighter than in the furnace of affliction."

The Lord teaches doctrine through *symbolic actions*. The Old Testament prophets employed a "show and tell" method for communicating God's message to His people. These actions were destined to teach them that God was faithful to His plan for them because His plan for them was designed to bring the Savior into the world to save the lost. Jeremiah wore an iron yoke around his neck to indicate that the Babylonian captivity would come to pass, and yet he preached that the people of God would return to their land. The Christ child was not to be born in Babylon but in Bethlehem. Hosea was commanded to marry Gomer, a prostitute, an employee of the "red light district." She was unfaithful to him and left him, breaking his heart. God was teaching him to relate to divine brokenheartedness. Hosea would never be able to preach passionately to the people of God who had been unfaithful to God and had broken God's heart until he "climbed into the *lav*, or heart, of God" and experienced for himself the unconditional love of God for God's people through personal brokenheartedness. God cannot love us more for the benevolent things that we do or love us less for the malevolent acts we commit. God only loves us because it is within His nature and character to do so.

God teaches doctrine through *types*. The Old Testament tabernacle is a graphic example of the relationship between God and God's people. The holy of holies was the compartment in the tabernacle into which the high priest went once a year on the Day of Atonement to offer a sacrifice of blood for the sins of the people. This had to be done year after year.

The old African American preacher picturesquely described this practice in terms of the contention between justice and mercy. Justice was growing weary of mercy making annual payments for the sparing of human creation. In Psalm 85:10, "Mercy and truth are met together, righteousness and peace have kissed each other." Mercy promised that the debt would be paid in full in the future. Finally, after forty-two generations, Jesus came. One day he died on the cross, and the veil was torn from top to bottom in the temple. In response, the poet Elvina M. Hall picked up her pen of inspiration and dipped it into the ink of illumination and wrote,

> Jesus paid it all,
> all to him I owe;
> sin had left a crimson stain,
> he washed it white as snow.[24]

God teaches doctrine through *analogy*. One of the classic analogical teaching demonstrations was the one used by Nathan to confront King David with his adulterous and murderous acts. John the Baptist had the same problem that Nathan's king, David,

24 Elvina M. Hall, "Jesus Paid It All," 1865.

had; that is, King Herod Antipas had also committed adultery. He had taken his brother Philip's wife. John the Baptist, without the use of analogy or indirection, directly approached Herod Antipas about this matter and ended up losing his head. Nathan, however, used an analogy of a wealthy livestock holder who took away the only lamb that the man had and served it as lamb chops for his unexpected guest. It was the "pet lamb" of the family. Nathan, the prophet, asked for David's response because the king was responsible for the execution of equity and justice in his domain. David was wroth and ended up indicting himself as he heard Nathan pronounce the chilling verdict of guilt: "You are the man, because you extinguished the life of Uriah, the husband of Bathsheba." The wealthy livestock holder was guilty of sheep stealing while the wealthy King David was guilty of wife stealing. The story was transformed into a mirror!

The story of Jesus and the Samaritan woman at the well is not just about water; it is a lens through which we see the heart of humanity. Jesus is teaching us that the heart of the matter of our human plight is a matter of the heart. The woman reveals *hardheartedness* in her assertion, "'How is it that You, being a Jew, ask a drink from me, a Samaritan woman?' For Jews have no dealings with Samaritans" (John 4:9 NKJV). She unveils human *shallow-heartedness* in her request, "Sir, give me this water, that I may not thirst, nor come here to draw" (v. 15). Jesus exposes human *crowded-heartedness* in his prophetic utterance, "You have had five husbands, and the man you now have is not your husband" (v. 18 NIV). She manifests *wholeheartedness* in believing in Jesus as the Messiah and going into the city and advertising for Jesus in her much-remembered testimony: "Come, see a man who told me everything I ever did. Could this be the Christ?" (v. 29 NIV).

Doctrinal preaching, more than any other kind of preaching, is likely to be heavy in complex, technical, and theological language. Jesus used parables to transmit His doctrine and to carry home His teachings. The parables are saturated with doctrine, but they are theology in pictures. A major element and ingredient in the Lord's doctrinal preaching and teaching ministry was His use of images. When Jesus used parables as a teaching device, He was essentially using secular stories, not Sunday school stories, to illustrate and unfold sacred secrets of the kingdom of God. These parables were designed to do more than inform the mind; they were intended to provide the hearers with a picture to hang on the walls in the gallery of their minds. Jesus told the parables to supply both visual and aural special effects; He wanted people to see and hear God, themselves, and others.

In his book *Preaching and Teaching with Imagination*, Warren W. Wiersbe succinctly promotes effective preaching as a process of turning windows into mirrors and ears into eyes; the people both hear and see what you're saying.[25] Jesus said, "Let the ones who have ears to hear, hear." Our prayer should be the one Elisha offered on behalf of his servant: "LORD, I pray thee, open his eyes, that he may see" (2 Kgs 6:17).

Jesus found analogies for the kingdom of heaven in soil, seed, leaven, fiscal transactions, wedding banquets, and trees that become lodging places for birds. The hearers always carried away a message after listening to Jesus, even though sometimes, like a medicinal time-release capsule, it was only after they were out of the presence of the great Teacher that it occurred to them that Jesus was speaking directly to them! The issue was left in the lap of the listeners. They were caught up in the middle of the action of a dramatic play without realizing that they were actors interacting with the main Actor of a divine drama. They were like Jacob who, after dreaming and hearing the Lord speak from the top of heaven's staircase, responded, "Surely the LORD is in this place; and I knew it not" (Gen 28:16).

This type of revelatory teaching enabled the hearers to encounter God and to experience the God who gives new perspectives

---

25 Warren W. Wiersbe, *Preaching and Teaching with Imagination* (Wheaton, IL: Victor, 1994), 6.

both to the events and emotions of our lives. The unconditional love of God is like a waiting father who keeps the calf fattened, sitting on the porch and looking down the road. He interrupts his son's apology when it moves into the territory of annulling the relationship between the father and the son and substitutes it for a master-servant relationship. He immediately moves to cover the returning son with a robe, honors him with a ring, and instantly calls for a celebration.

God's love is like a shepherd leaving ninety-nine of His sheep in the wilderness, not in a secure barn, searching for the one lost sheep until it is found and carrying the bruised and injured sheep across the rugged terrain of the wilderness until He brings it into the safe haven of His territory. He welcomes the community to rejoice with Him. God's love is like a woman who loses one of ten coins in her house, sweeps the floor, looks in every corner, moves every piece of furniture around, turns the house upside down until the coin is found, and puts it back into the bag with the other nine. She invites the community to celebrate with her.

Jesus even used a picture to describe hell. To a society without electricity, Jesus depicted hell as "outer darkness." He also portrayed hell, or *gehenna*, as a garbage dump where the worms ate the garbage and the fires smoldered. As a contrast, Jesus imaged heaven as a banquet attended by those who accepted the gracious and inexplicable invitation of the Lord. Donald Grey Barnhouse used to say, "Everyone goes to heaven God's way or goes to hell their own way."

The great German theologian preacher, Helmut Thielicke, demonstrated an insightful principle from Jesus' healing of the man born blind. Our encounter with Christ precedes our reflection on that experience. This biblical story helped Thielicke understand that proclamation precedes doctrine and theology. We hear the gospel and are saved, and we later reflect on the experience and meaning of the proclamation. When people become believers and are saved, they go to Bible study to try to understand doctrinally and theologically what happened at the moment of their conversion and how it happened. The words of one great song,

> Something happened and now I know;
> He touched me and made me whole,

reinforce this argument.[26] The blind man was healed by Jesus, who encountered him. He was not qualified to give a doctrinal and theological reflection of his experience with Christ. Instead, he admitted to his interrogators, "Whether he is a sinner or not I don't know." He knew that he had an experience with Christ, for he confessed to them, "I was blind but now I see" (John 9:25 NIV). But it was not until Christ presented Himself to the man as the Messiah that the newly sighted man comprehended who the healer was and could give an informed doctrinal and theological response. Now, as a result of his belief, he could say more than "a man they call Jesus" (v. 11); he could also say, "Lord, I believe" (v. 38). The preacher of doctrine would do well to follow the Lord's method.

One of the ways that Paul presented doctrine was through the use of thoroughly secular images in declaring the central mysteries of the gospel. When Paul spoke of redemption, he was associating it with culture and giving it doctrinal content. The death and resurrection of the second Adam bought back the children of the first Adam who were enslaved to Satan. One of the greatest little doctrinal passages or sections in the Bible is the book of Philemon. Paul admonishes Philemon to receive Onesimus, the runaway slave, as Philemon would receive Paul as a brother. This was an act of mercy, for mercy is withholding the death that we deserve. A runaway slave deserved to die, but he was given a chance to live.

---

26 William J. Gaither, "He Touched Me," William J. Gaither, Inc. ARR UBP of Gaither Copyright Management, 1964. Permission granted.

David foreshadowed this great Pauline doctrine of grace and mercy when he affirmed, "Surely goodness (*hesed* in the Hebrew language is the word for "loving-kindness" or "loyal love") and mercy shall follow me all the days of my life: and I will dwell in the house of the LORD forever" (Ps 23:6). Prolific author Warren W. Wiersbe has said, "When we stand before the Lord and look behind us, there will be no acts of sin in our past because goodness and mercy have been following us and cleaning up behind us."[27] In the words of the great hymnist, we will be "dressed in His righteousness alone, faultless to stand before the throne."[28]

When Paul instructed Philemon to charge Onesimus's reception as a brother to his account, he was offering an image of the doctrine of imputed righteousness. Onesimus, who was still legally a slave, was to be received as a brother in Christ. Paul was saying that he would bear the debt, but Philemon was to accept Onesimus.

Paul used *benedictions* to teach doctrine. The oft-repeated benediction, "The grace of the Lord Jesus Christ, and the love of God, and the communion of the Holy Ghost, be with you all" (2 Cor 13:14), brings us face-to-face with the reality of a Trinity of divine persons. As far as God as Father is concerned, I was saved when He chose me in Christ, declared in preexistent eternity (I didn't know anything about it). As far as God as Son is concerned, I was saved when Christ died for me on the cross, confirmed in history (I heard about it, and I believed it). As far as God as Holy Spirit is concerned, I was saved when I was regenerated by the Spirit, personalized in my lifetime (I experienced this without comprehending it). Dwight L. Moody's theology of preaching can be measured by a trinity of realities: humans were ruined by the fall, redeemed by the blood, and regenerated by the Spirit. The

---

27 A conversation with Warren W. Wiersbe, August 10, 2004, Lincoln, NE.
28 Edward Mote, "The Solid Rock," 1836.

great Pauline Trinitarian doctrine antiphonally resounds with the hymnic lyrics, "God in three persons; blessed Trinity."[29]

Paul taught the priesthood of all believers. He expanded the Old Testament office of the priesthood and pictured the body of Christ as a royal priesthood. He would not agree with today's dichotomy of the clergy and the laity. He preached and taught that all believers are priests unto God, ministers to one another in relationship with the entire church of God, and they enter into the presence of the great high priest, Jesus Christ. Believers do the work together.

Paul was constantly borrowing images from the secular world, emptying them of their original content and refilling them with doctrinal solution that reflected central truths of Scripture. For Paul, the sport of wrestling was seen as spiritual warfare with principalities, powers, rulers of the darkness of this world, and spiritual wickedness in high places (Eph 6:12). The athletic competition of running a race was envisioned as a dedicated effort to participate in the Christian race according to the regulations of the Word of God and the constant concentration of keeping one's attention on Jesus, the author and finisher of our faith (Heb 12:1–2). Paul used a term from the accounting field and transformed its original secular meaning into one that clearly showed that whatever a believer forsakes for the cause of Christ is dung or waste in comparison to being found in Christ. Paul was extremely effective in contemporizing secular terms from various fields in order to demonstrate doctrinal truths and realities.

The apostle John, in the book of Revelation, used the glossary of Old Testament terms and through the employment of "sermonic eschatonics" gave us a panorama of eternity as he forecasted the redeemed in their glorified state as creation is delivered from the groaning and travail of the effects of the fall (Rom 8:22). At that time, "henceforth" will change places with "hitherto"; the "already" will be swallowed up into the "not yet"; faith will surrender to the

29 Reginald Heber, "Holy, Holy, Holy," 1826.

reign of sight; the incomplete will be completed by the Complete One; and we, who have in past times seen "through a glass darkly," will see "face to face." In the Old Testament, the Hebrew term for seeing "face to face" is *panim a panim*. It referred to transparency and the removal of barriers. This is what the Scriptures have in mind when they announce that the Lord spoke to Moses "face to face, as a man speaks to his friend" (Exod 33:11 ESV). The ultimate goal of all doctrine is not to be informed about Bible facts but to be transformed by being in relationship with the person of Jesus Christ. One day believers will see the One they have been taught about. The apostle John, in Revelation 1, pictures Jesus as the great high priest in all of His glory and succinctly anticipates our eschatological *panim a panim* experience: "And they shall see his face" (Rev 22:4). And Lord, haste the day when my faith shall be sight!

As doctrinal preachers, we need to be liberated from the sterile and predictable language used in our preaching. This language is more like dusting plastic flowers than cultivating roses. The doctrinal preacher needs to use language that is similar to the language of the Bible—language that has elasticity and portability for use in our contemporary times. Doctrine does not come to us from some esoteric arena; rather, it emerges from the seams of society. Phillips Brooks said, "Preaching is the communication of truth by man to men."[30] He would have contended that the preacher must discover the place where truth and life intersect.

Doctrine is found in life, and life is found in doctrine. Doctrine reaches into the nitty-gritty and raw places. It reaches into the bruised and battered places. It travels to the innermost recesses of the soul. It makes its way through the narrow places of human existence. This does not mean that the traditional doctrinal words and images need to be discarded and jettisoned, and a new and fresh set of doctrinal words and images used in their places. Doctrinal terms like *propitiation, justification, sanctification,*

---

30 Phillips Brooks, *Lectures on Preaching* (New York: Dutton, 1877), 5.

glorification, grace, and *justice* represent the terminological coinage of the church. When a United States citizen travels to a foreign country, that citizen has to exchange the currency of the United States for the currency of that country if they are to do business in that country. But when the time comes for that citizen to return to the United States, he or she has to convert the foreign currency back into U.S. currency if financial transactions are to be executed within the United States of America.

Doctrinal preachers need to retain the traditional *doctrinal dictionary* because the definitions of those terms are paralleled in God's Word. While preaching may make adaptations to the traditional *doctrinal vocabulary* in order to communicate doctrinal truths to a biblically illiterate contemporary audience, the biblical text must always be allowed to voice the author's original intent. A text can never mean today what it never meant when it was originally written and spoken. The human predicament is the same as it was when our first parents sinned in the garden of Eden.

Life is made up of lament and laughter, pain and pleasure, ascent and descent. Solomon poetically captured the antitheses of life in Ecclesiastes 3:1–2: "To every thing there is a season, and a time to every purpose under the heaven: a time to be born and a time to die." Doctrinal preachers must teach doctrine the way the Lord taught doctrine: engaging the minds of people with familiar language that made the strange doctrinal concepts seem terribly familiar to their deepest desires, longings, and fears. God used spokespersons in the Bible to go into the taperoom of human existence, rewind the tape through personal address, and replay the tape through personal witness so that the listeners would hear their own story in the communication and exclaim, "This is my story, this is my song." People must hear the doctrine as the Jews from all over the then-known world heard the Pentecostal message; they heard it in their own languages (Acts 2:6). This Pentecostal sermon evoked and produced dialogue. The way God taught doctrine in the Bible produced dialogue.

Chapter Four

THE PREACHER AS AN EXEGETICAL ESCORT

A metaphor is an extension of meaning which represents something by comparing one thing to another. Essentially it is an image. I had been searching for an image with a fresh homiletical picture, a visual that was fresh and functional, which could carry the text.

In Search of a Substantive Homiletical Metaphor

There are a lot of metaphors in homiletical literature. Jana Childers's book *Performing the Word*[1] uses the theatrical-performance metaphor for preaching a first-person narrative sermon. Kirk Byron Jones's book *The Jazz of Preaching*[2] uses jazz as a metaphor for preaching. Eugene Lowry's book *The Homiletical Plot*[3] uses the metaphor of a plot for preaching a narrative sermon. Richard Eslinger's book *The Web of Preaching*[4] offers the metaphor of a web as an image for exploring the interconnectivity of various homiletical strategies and styles for preaching. I searched for an integrating and controlling metaphor that would embody within its bosom the essence of preaching: substance. I found it in the escort metaphor.

The exegetical escort is one who ushers hearers into the presence of God for the purpose of transformation. Once the exegetical escort has ushered hearers into the presence of God and given them the Word, the escort's job is over. The escort leaves them in the throne room of God and lets God transform them.

1 Jana Childers, *Performing the Word* (Nashville: Abingdon, 1988).
2 Kirk Byron Jones, *The Jazz of Preaching* (Nashville: Abingdon, 2004).
3 Eugene Lowry, *The Homiletical Plot* (Atlanta: John Knox, 1980).
4 Richard Eslinger, *The Web of Preaching* (Nashville: Abingdon, 2002).

But the escort metaphor has a sinister semantic. It evokes and calls forth the thought of an escort service, suggestive of a purveyor of sexual services. I had to sanctify the escort metaphor and baptize it before I entered it into the sacred service of the biblical text. This metaphor has sanction from Scripture for use in preaching. It is a biblical metaphor. Galatians 3:24 provides the word *paidagogos*, which means "tutor" and/or "trainer." It says, "The Law served as a tutor." The Law served as a schoolmaster that escorted or ushered us to Christ. Preachers become, for the people in churches, escorts who take the Word and usher them into the presence of God as a *paidagogos* for the purpose of transformation.

Exegesis is the science of drawing out of the text the meaning that is in the text. The preacher must return to the original meaning of the text and make an application for today. So an exegetical escort takes the meaning in the text and ushers people by the Word. The text serves as the manual that provides directions for entering into the presence of God for the purpose of transformation. Preachers of the Word are exegetical escorts and must be diligent students of the Word of God. As students of the Word, preachers search for what God's Word really says in its raw radiance without denominationalizing, ethnicizing, culturalizing, fossilizing, minimizing, maximizing, trivializing, or sanitizing the text. They take the original meaning of the text—the text as it is, even though it cuts, confronts, and challenges both the preacher of the Word and the hearers to whom the Word is preached.

They are called to show forth the praises of Him who has called them out of darkness into the marvelous light. They are called to be witnesses. Acts 1:8 says, "But you will receive power when the Holy Spirit has come upon you, and you will be my witnesses in Jerusalem and in all Judea and Samaria, and to the ends of the earth" (ESV). They do not have the luxury of saying, "It goes without saying." When it relates to the Scripture, nothing "goes without saying." Preachers must thoroughly relate the truth of Scripture and cannot assume that the people understand it. Years ago they could give congregations a portion of a biblical story, and they could finish the story. Preachers would say, "You know the story." They could quote half of the Scripture passage, and the people would quote the rest of it. Today there is widespread biblical illiteracy in the church. The preacher must tell the story and not assume that it is known by members of the church.

The Double Trajectory of Preaching

There is a double trajectory in preaching: the prophetic trajectory and the priestly trajectory. The ministry of the priest is preferred to that of a prophet because the prophet afflicts the comfortable and the priest comforts the afflicted. The priest asks, "Is there no balm in Gilead? Is there no physician there?" The priest gives spiritual medicine and spiritual massages. Jesus the priest invites, "Come unto me, all ye that labor and are heavy laden, and I will give you rest" (Matt 11:28). Instead of the priest offering a balm, the prophet indicts the people and delivers a bomb to those who are at ease in Zion. Preachers need to know when and how to use the *bomb* and the *balm*, depending upon whether people who are afflicted need to be comforted or whether people who are comfortable need to be afflicted. Preaching must have a double trajectory where the text speaks both a priestly and prophetic word.

Outward Projection and Inward Appropriation

As exegetical escorts, we often carry the Word for the benefit of others. We always have a word for the church. Wouldn't it be strange on Sunday morning for the pastors to say to their Sunday morning congregations, "The service is cancelled for lack of a word from God?" The challenge for preachers is to have a word from

God for themselves! Wouldn't it be unimaginable and unthinkable for a gas truck to be stranded on the side of the road? A gas truck has two tanks, one for the station it is delivering gas to and the other for the fueling of its own engine. The gas truck might be full of gas for its regular deliveries, but it is not going anywhere because its own personal gas tank is empty. Preachers of the Word cannot afford to run out of gas because their own spiritual vitality is at stake. They cannot entertain the possibility of even running on fumes. The result is personal dryness and emptiness.

We are cracked pots serving as depositories for the treasure of the gospel (2 Cor 4:7). Do you know what God has done? He has given us a diamond message and placed it in a casing that is cracked and unworthy of housing the diamond. Billy Graham appeared on *Larry King Live* prior to his June 2005 New York Evangelistic Crusade. During the interview Graham stated that when he gets to heaven he is going to ask God, "Why did you choose me? There is nothing special about me." He has preached to more people than any other human being. When you and I get to heaven, we will probably ask the same question: Why did you choose me? We are just cracked pots. We are not worthy of God's blessing. There is nothing special about us. If we are special, it is because we serve a special and great God. But innately and inherently, there is nothing special about us. That is why worship ought to be spontaneous. It ought to be a lifestyle and not just an event. Our permanent residence should be within the atmosphere of worship. The psalmist said in Psalm 139:6, "Such knowledge is too wonderful for me." We are just cracked pots and yet God has chosen to use us.

Preaching to the Disinclined

We preach to some people who are disinclined and do not want to hear God's Word. Some congregations tend to be more cardiological (heart people) than cranial (head people). Some congregations want to feel more than think, and others want to think more than feel. For the exegetical escort it is not an either-or dynamic; rather, it is a both-and dynamic.

Isaiah's question in Isaiah 53:1 is a pertinent question for the twenty-first-century pulpit: "Who hath believed our report? and to whom is the arm of the Lord revealed?" Have our congregations really believed our report? The question asked in the text is not "Who has heard our report?" The question is, "Who hath believed our report?" Jeremiah 8:22 depicts Jeremiah's struggle with the resistance to his message. At the outset he did not want to preach. In chapter 1 he had said to God, "I am too young." God said, "No, do not say you are too young. In fact, I called you even before you were conceived in the womb, and ordained you to be a prophet to the nations." Now Jeremiah's message is resisted not only by his family of priests but also the prophets and the kings. In chapter 20, verse 7, he even said, "God has tricked me." Everyone is against him. So in Jeremiah 8:22, he asks, "Is there no physician there?" He is referring to his prophetic proclamation. He had been teaching and proclaiming all those years, and it looked like there was no medicine to heal and no physician to correct what was wrong. After all, the priests, the prophets, and the king were against him, and it seemed like God had not stopped by to validate what he had proclaimed.

Jesus was talking about Himself and John the Baptist when He said, "We played the flute for you, and you did not dance; we sang a dirge, and you did not cry" (Luke 7:32 NIV). Jesus was saying, "Whatever John and I do, you are determined not to accept our message." If preachers today are going to be effective exegetical escorts, we must anticipate that there will be people in the congregation who will not accept the message of Scripture.

Some of the disciples once said to Jesus, "This is an hard saying; who can hear it?" (John 6:60). As a result of the nonnegotiable teaching, many of the at-large disciples walked with Him no more. Jesus turned to the twelve disciples and asked, "Will you also go?" It was as if Jesus were saying, "I do not need you either. You can go on and leave." Peter spoke for the twelve and said, "To whom shall we go? Thou hast the words of eternal life" (v. 68). Some of Jesus' followers left Him because of His doctrine. Some of the people in today's congregations will reject the truth of the biblical message.

A Diagnosis and Prognosis for Preaching

Robert Moats Miller's biography *Harry Emerson Fosdick: Preacher, Pastor and Prophet* records the words of a Roman Catholic observer who once predicted that if Protestantism ever dies with a dagger in its back, the dagger will be the Protestant sermon.[5] Unfortunately, too much of our preaching is like the art of embalming the dead and then decking out the dead on Sunday morning in the midst of crowds as if the corpse were still alive. Preaching is serious. I recall the words of Augustine: "For Thou has created us for Thyself, and our heart cannot be quieted till it may find repose in Thee."[6] And since that is the case, we must remember that every time we attempt to preach it as if we were writing with a piece of chalk on the minds of people. We need chalk because there are things that need to be erased, corrected, and rewritten in our preaching. Our proclamation needs to be washed in the fluid of forgiveness.

I want to offer a diagnosis of preaching and present the biblical exegetical escort, Jesus Christ. What is the matter with preaching today? First, there is *the dilution of grace*. Paul in his writings always put a theology of grace before a theology of works. Doctrine always preceded deeds. In Romans 1–11 he talks about the grace of justification, sanctification, glorification, adoption, and the like. When he comes to Romans 8:31 he

5 Robert Moats Miller, *Harry Emerson Fosdick: Preacher, Pastor and Prophet* (New York: Oxford University Press, 1985), 334–35.
6 Augustine, *Confessions*, trans. William Watts (Cambridge, MA: Harvard University Press, 1998), 3.

asks: "What shall we say to these things?" "These things" refer to all the doctrines of grace preceding this verse. And then he goes on to talk about election and predestination in chapters 9–11. In chapter 12 he opens up, "Brethren, I beseech you by the mercies of God," mercies that are visible in the first eleven chapters. Furthermore, he discusses the service gifts from the end of chapter 12 through chapter 16. These are ethical deeds and responsibilities. The same scenario occurs in Ephesians. Chapter 1:1–13 is really just one uninterrupted verse where trinitarian presence is inserted. In addition, he focuses on predestination and election, and the height and depth and breadth and wisdom of the love of God. Finally he comes to 4:1 where he says, "As a prisoner of the Lord . . . I urge you to live a life worthy of the calling you have received" (NIV). Paul's area of concentration in chapters 4–6 is ethics. It is always theology before ethics and doctrine before deeds.

Anselm talked about faith seeking understanding. It is not Anselm's intention to get Christians to understand and get all the facts right so that they can be theologically sound in their thought and reflection; rather, the direction is moving an inquirer of Christ from a need to believe in order to understand. It is believing in order to understand.

Martin Luther lifted up the indicative above the imperative. The indicative is who I am; the imperative is what I must do as a result of who I am. It is not the imperative first: I must do this in order to become a Christian. Rather, it is the indicative first: because I am a Christian, I do what I do. I do not work toward salvation; I work from salvation. The love of Christ constrains me.

Dietrich Bonhoeffer in his book *The Cost of Discipleship*[7] mentions "cheap grace"; this is grace without any accompanying ethical and social responsibility. There is something worse than cheap

---

7 Dietrich Bonhoeffer, *The Cost of Discipleship* (New York: Collier, Macmillan, 1973), 45.

grace; it is perverted grace, grace that is stretched so that it is no longer grace.

One of my Beeson Divinity School preaching students, Robbie Grames, admits that he loves sweet tea and does not like to put ice in it because ice dilutes the tea. He likes to put his tea in the refrigerator because he wants the tea to emit full-body flavor. He has gone to other countries where they do not initially serve ice; ice has to be requested. He says that he likes to drink his iced tea straight.

When it comes to grace, one has to drink it straight. One cannot add anything to it. Too often in our preaching we start off with justification by grace; then after people get saved, we move on to preaching sanctification by works. If I am saved by grace, then I am sanctified by grace. I cannot add anything to it. It is grace plus nothing—*not* grace plus my achievement, merits, works, or credentials; it is grace plus nothing. I want my grace sweet the way John Newton expressed it in his rendition: "Amazing grace how *sweet* the sound." And my preaching must reflect the Alpha and Omega of a grace grip.

Second, there is *the eclipse of the cross.* In Hebrews 5:8, Jesus the Son of God learned "obedience from what he suffered." The Son of God had to experience discipline to be obedient through suffering. This is the sinless and infinite One. We are not allowed to skip a theology of the cross and move immediately to a theology of glory. John Fischer wrote a book titled *On a Hill Too Far Away.*[8] The cross has been moved out of the way in our preaching. The cross has become too distant from our preaching. A. W. Tozer diagnosed preaching by its allegiance to the "old cross" or the "new cross." He argues: "All unannounced and mostly undetected there has come in modern times a new cross into popular evangelical circles. It is like the old cross but different: the likenesses are superficial; the differences, fundamental. From this new cross has sprung a new philosophy of the Christian life, and from that new

8 John Fischer, *On a Hill Too Far Away* (Minneapolis, MN: Bethany, 2001).

philosophy has come a new evangelical technique—a new type of meeting and a new kind of preaching."[9]

The cross is so central in salvation history that the only thing Elijah and Moses talked about as heavenly delegates to the summit meeting at the transfiguration of Christ was the *exodon*, or death at Jerusalem (Luke 9:31). Elijah, who represented the prophets, and Moses, who represented the law, appeared with Christ as if to declare that Christ was the fulfillment of both the law and the prophets. It seemed as if the concern of heaven was the cross. "I love to tell the story; 'twill be my theme in glory." Shouldn't the cross be our theme on earth as well? The *theologia crucis* has been replaced by the *theologia gloria*. Martin Luther criticized the scholastics for having solely a theology of achievement, triumph, and attainment and not one of suffering. There is no resurrection without a crucifixion. When I go back to the cross, I see some things that I had not seen before. At the cross God came as close as He ever came to writing His name. Here at the cross the greatest transaction in human history took place. I used to think that there were just two thieves at the cross, but German theologian Helmut Thielicke helped me to see differently. Just as Nebuchadnezzar saw an additional man, the fourth man, in the fiery furnace, I saw an additional thief on the cross. I needed to get my math right. There was one on the left and another one on the right. But there is also a thief in the middle.

First Thessalonians 5:2 (NIV) declares, "The day of the Lord will come like a thief"; Revelation 3:3 (NIV) asserts, "I will come like a thief"; and Revelation 16:15 states, "Behold, I will come as a thief." There is a third thief, and He is in the middle. Paul says He took something from me. "What things were gain to me, those I counted loss for Christ" (Phil 3:7). Paul is saying, "What he took from me, I counted it as dung, *skebula*, human excrement, human

---

9 A. W. Tozer, *Man the Dwelling Place of God* (Harrisburg, PA: Christian Publications, 1966), 42.

refuse. He is a thief who comes to take from you and give you something of eternal value."

Jim Elliot, martyred for the sake of the gospel, was referring to this "better exchange" when he wrote, "He is no fool who gives what he cannot keep to gain that which he cannot lose."[10] Jesus was talking about making sure that His followers were not bankrupt in heaven. He said, "Do not store up for yourselves treasures on earth, where moth and rust destroy, and where thieves break in and steal. But store up for yourselves treasures in heaven, where moth and rust do not destroy, and where thieves do not break in and steal" (Matt 6:19–20 NIV). Jesus takes what we have committed to Him that is transferable and transforms it into heavenly assets. He is a thief!

George Matheson, the Scottish hymnist, says:

> Lord, make me a captive and I shall be free;
> Take away my sword and I shall conqueror be.[11]

We are only free when we are His captives, and we only conquer when we are defenseless. Psalm 46:10 reads, "Be still and know that I am God." The essence of this verse is not motionlessness or voicelessness; it is defenselessness. This psalm can be interpreted as God saying, "As you stand before your enemy, strip yourself and stand there defenseless so that you depend upon me for deliverance." The battle is not ours; it is the Lord's.

The nineteenth-century Scottish preacher and pastor Alexander Whyte often used this phrase in his pastoral prayers: "Lord, I give myself to thee, and whatever I cannot give I invite you to take." There are things that are so ingrained and entrenched in believers, and which have coalesced and hardened in time—habits, temperaments, attitudes, some demeanors. They must invite Christ to take what they cannot give. The greatest theft in human history took place in a cemetery where Jesus took the sting out of

10 Elisabeth Elliot, *In the Shadow of the Almighty* (New York: Harper & Row, 1958), 15.
11 George Matheson, "Make Me a Captive, Lord," 1890.

death, robbed the grave of its victory, and declared all power was in his hand. The Christological thief has come to take our darkness and give us light; take our brokenness and give us wholeness; take our poverty and give us true riches; take our despair and give us joy.

Third, there is *a demise of doctrine*. The greatest divorce to take place in the church in the last fifty years is the divorce between the minister of music and the minister of Christian education. And what is so sad is that the pastor has officiated over the ceremony. The minister of Christian education and the minister of music need to be remarried. They were not divorced in the early church. In Acts 2:41 we learn that three thousand souls were added to the church, and God continued to add to the church daily those who were being saved. Verse 42 states, "And they continued steadfastly in the apostles' doctrine." This is Christian education. Verse 47 adds that they continually praised God. This is Christian worship.

The pastor is the resident theologian and must inform the minister of Christian education and the minister of music that regardless of the meter and the rhythm of a song, the message must be theological and biblical. In our churches we sing more heresies than the early church councils ever condemned during the patristic period. Worshippers may do musicological flips and liturgical calisthenics, but heaven will not bless untheological and unbiblical songs. There is no antithesis between musical inspiration and biblical lyrics. The minister of Christian education prepares students for the sermon and the minister of music prepares worshippers to worship God biblically and intelligently. The church fathers used to confess their beliefs. Today we believe the confessions of the church fathers. The next generation will probably just confess the confessions of the church fathers. We must preach and teach so that people become biblically literate. Many people in the church do not know what they believe. Many seminarians know what they believe but do not know why they believe what they believe. A generation needs to be raised up that says, I

85

know what and why I believe, and then I know whom I believe. Paul says, "I know whom I have believed, and am persuaded that he is able to keep that which I have committed unto him against that day" (2 Tim 1:12).

Fourth, there is *the disconnection between traditional theological language and contemporary relevant imagery.* Theology is not the faith; it is talk about the faith. Harry Emerson Fosdick said, "Astronomies change but the stars abide."[12] God never changes, but our studies and perspectives about God do change. So we have to come to the place where we talk about God differently today from the way God was referred to fifty years ago. Some members have no church background. People come off the streets who have never picked up a Bible. They are often bombarded with these theological words—*justification, sanctification, propitiation, glorification,* and the like. They do not understand these terms. We must not jettison or discard traditional theological terms. They must be rebaptized in the solution of contemporary relevance. The traditional theological dictionary must remain the same while the contemporary relevant vocabulary and terminology correspond to the precise meaning of the biblical and theological terms.

How does the preacher talk about the concept of depravity or Adamic sin in the twenty-first century? Using the language of addiction, a newborn is addicted to crack because the baby was conceived and delivered during the nine-month period in which the birth mother consistently took crack cocaine. The baby did nothing to become an addict; the baby just inherited an addiction from the mother. Adam was a sin addict, and the human race inherited a sin addiction from him. The second Adam, Christ, came to take the sin predicament by becoming what we were— sin! The theological word *depravity* is exchanged for the more relevant, comprehensible term *addiction* without sacrificing the

---

12 Harry Emerson Fosdick, paraphrasing his mentor, William Newton Clarke, http://www.fpcnyc.org/influences.html, accessed May 16, 2007.

original theological intention. A word must mean what it means, not what we want it to mean.

How does one talk about redemption? I am an African American, but experientially I do not know anything about slavery. I have never been to a slave auction block and talked to an actual slave. How does one talk about 1 Peter 1:18–19 without the actual experience of slavery? "Ye were not redeemed with corruptible things, as silver and gold, from your vain conversation received by tradition from your fathers; but with the precious blood of Christ, as of a lamb without blemish and without spot." How do we talk about redemption when we do not know what slavery is? But people know what a hostage is. A loved one is kidnapped and held as a hostage. The relative has to come up with a certain amount of money, and until they do, the loved one will be held as a hostage or be killed if the money is not received by the kidnapper.

The devil kidnapped the human race and held it hostage. Psalm 85:10 states, "Mercy and truth are met together; righteousness and peace have kissed each other." A conference was held in heaven, and God decided that the only way the ransom note could be paid was not for God to send someone but for God to send Himself. That is what the incarnation is all about. God came from God: "The Word was made flesh, and dwelt among us, (and we beheld his glory, the glory of the only begotten of the Father), full of grace and truth" (John 1:14). God had made a promise in Genesis 3:15, the first promise of redemption through Jesus Christ, the seed of a woman. A promissory note was presented once a year during the Day of Atonement; a lamb was slain as a sign of God's forgiveness of the sins of the Israelites for the whole year and as a foreshadowing of the lamb of God who would come to take away the sin of the world (John 1:29). On Friday the God who came in the flesh in the incarnation died on the cross as the "crucified God." The veil in the temple was torn from top to bottom; God was tearing up the ransom note. We must keep the meaning of traditional theological language while transitioning to a contemporary vocabulary and terminology that hearers can appropriate and understand.

Fifth, there is *the dissemination of anthropocentric preaching.* We have been affected by the past. During the Renaissance, there was an emphasis on the inversion of a human being. In human thought God was replaced by a human being as the center of the universe. This is particularly true in the thinking of the seventeenth-century scientist René Descartes, whose dictum was, "I think, therefore I am" (*cogito ergo sum*). Our preaching is becoming more human centered than God centered. Bryan Chapell decries the rise of humanism in a concept he calls *sola bootstrapsa*: "Pull yourself up by your own bootstraps."

> Humpty Dumpty sat on a wall,
> Humpty Dumpty had a great fall.
> All the king's horses and all the king's men
> Could not put Humpty together again.

But I know a King who can! He is the King of kings and the Lord of lords. Bryan Chapell challenges preachers to look at their congregations as a piece of swiss cheese when they stand before them to preach the Word of God. Both the preacher and the people have holes in them, and only the Word of God can fill the holes and make them complete. Second Timothy 3:16–17 says, "All Scripture is given by inspiration of God, and is profitable for doctrine, for reproof, for correction, for instruction in righteousness: that the man of God may be perfect, throughly furnished unto all good works."

God gave us the Ten Commandments and knew we could not keep them. Our inability to keep the regulations (prohibitions) reveals something about the character of humans and the character of the divine. The regulation, "Thou shalt not lie", reveals something about our character: we are dishonest. It also reveals something about God's character. God is a God of integrity and honesty. Since God is what we are not, only God can fill that hole and make us what we ought to be. Jesus is the antithesis of the last six regulations of the Ten Commandments. He is truth. When we look in the Bible, we have to see ourselves as being unable to change ourselves. Thomas à Kempis wrote, "Make possible to me, O Lord, by grace what seemeth impossible to me by nature."[13] A lot of humanistic preaching is going forth from the pulpit, for preachers tell their parishioners to reach down inside of themselves and find the power to sustain themselves through any trial. If that is the case, then Christ came in vain because He came to do for us what we could not do for ourselves. We must not let this bleed into our preaching because it causes our preaching to become thin and watered down. A recent book by Dr. E. K. Bailey, *Farther in and Deeper Down*, provides a title that destroys the myth of many self-help books and the message of humorous televangelists.[14] Only God can reach farther in and go deeper down to put the interiority of the human state in order.

Sixth, there is *detachment of the mystery of God from the revelation of God*. Martin Luther referred to the concealing of God as *deus absconditus* and the revealing of God as *deus revelatus*. God made humans in His own image and after His likeness. Some modern preaching is attempting to reverse the process so that the mystery of God is demystified and the inscrutability of God is unscrewed. William Cowper, the British hymnist wrote,

> God moves in a mysterious way
> His wonders to perform;
> He plants His footsteps in the sea
> and rides upon the storm.[15]

God reserves the right to reveal Himself and to be inconspicuous. God is the God of the beyond. Too many of our modern-day preachers pose as if they were so familiar with God that they

13 Thomas à Kempis, *The Imitation of Christ*, trans. William Benham, Harvard Classics (New York: Collier, 1909), 3:19.
14 E. K. Bailey, *Farther in and Deeper Down* (Chicago: Moody, 2005).
15 William Cowper, "God Moves in a Mysterious Way," 1774.

receive advance heavenly bulletins that notify them of what His next move will be. Too often preachers posture themselves to be in such an intimate relationship with God that they have regularly scheduled press conferences with the Holy One and conduct dialogues with Deity in heaven. They pretend to have come back from heaven with quick fixes for human problems and clear answers for complex issues. This kind of preaching blurs the distinction between the transcendence of God (God above us) and the immanence of God (God with us).

This type of preaching erases the distance between mystery and revelation in Deity. God chooses to drape Himself in mystery. No wonder the psalmist declares, "Thy way is in the sea, and thy path in the great waters, and thy footsteps are not known" (Ps 77:19). Paul confirms the psalmist's assertion: "O the depth of the riches both of the wisdom and knowledge of God! how unsearchable are his judgments and his ways past finding out!" (Rom 11:33). Would we want to serve a God about whom there was no mystery? He remains in the realm of mystery, and we worship Him as Lord; yet He steps out of mystery into the arena of revelation in the person of Jesus, and we relate to Him as our elder brother. We are allowed a peek at the mystery of God through Jesus, who is the human face of God. He told the disciples, "Anyone who has seen me has seen the Father" (John 14:9 NIV). The scenes at the baptism and transfiguration of Jesus offered momentary glimpses of the mystery of God. In the eschaton, mystery will surrender itself in the arms of revelation, for the quest of the saints of all the ages will be fulfilled: "They shall see his face" (Rev 22:4). We must not reduce the God of mystery to a God who always immediately speaks, acts, and solves our problems. We must not play God with our hearers. We can be confident that if we proclaim the revealed truth of God's Word, God's voice will be heard and a response will be evoked (even if it is one of rejection). We can also find solace that in eternity God will provide future grace for earth's unanswered questions and unsolved problems. For decades Christians have been singing,

We are tossed and driv'n on the restless sea of time;
Somber skies and howling tempest oft succeed a
bright sunshine,
In that land of perfect day, when the mists are rolled
away,
We will understand it better by and by.[16]

Only when faith yields to sight, the hitherto surrenders to the henceforth, and the "more" of devastation embraces the "no more" of eternity's delights will we no longer see through a glass darkly, but rather see face-to-face. Until then preachers must keep them in tension, for what God has joined together is not to be separated!

A Biblical Survey of the Exegetical Escort

The Bible abounds with images, nuances, and examples of the dynamic of the exegetical escort. This metaphor not only has the potential for making a significant contribution to homiletical literature; it also has biblical precedence and support. Being a servant to the text is its primary role. It is designed to involve itself in the interpretation of the text without usurping the authority of the text. If this metaphor seeks to become the master of the text instead of being content to be the servant of the text, it has forgotten its role.

The prophet-priest Ezekiel sat by the river of Chebar at Tel-abib with the Jewish exiles during the Babylonian captivity. He did what is extremely difficult for any preacher: he remained silent for seven days as he experienced the despair of the captives and absorbed their pain. He was participating in empathetic listening. He had nothing to say to them because he had not received a word from the Lord for them. Inferentially, Ezekiel instructs the twenty-first-century preacher that people will show concern for the preacher's Sunday sermon if the preacher shows concern for the people during the week. After the seven days had expired, the

---

16 Charles A. Tindley, "We'll Understand It Better By and By," 1905.

Lord summoned Ezekiel to come to the plain for a conference. The conference was really a magnificent monologue, for God did all the talking! God talked from 3:22 to 11:12. The word of the Lord continuously came to Ezekiel, and he remained silent as he did for the seven days sitting with the Jewish exiles. Ezekiel had not preached for quite a while. He had the wisdom to know that a preacher has nothing to say to the people until God has spoken to the preacher. After listening to the people for seven days and to God for eight chapters, Ezekiel finally had something of significance to say, for he begins to prophesy in 11:13. He has been escorted into the presence of God for information and proceeds to escort the Jewish exiles into the presence of God through the Word of God, which he has received from God. His escorting them by the Word of God encouraged the captives to trust in the God who promised that a remnant of Jews would return to Jerusalem and rebuild the temple and city. They were transformed by these words, and under Zerubbabel and others they would return and rebuild.

Ezra the priest was faced with a great challenge. The returned exiles had not kept the annual Passover during their captivity and had not been hearing and reading the Word of God. During the rebuilding of Jerusalem and the reconstruction of the walls, Ezra assembled the Jews for a worship service, and he stood up in a pulpit and read the Word of God to the people for several hours. He was assisted in the task of proclamation by Levites who went throughout the congregation explaining to the people what the texts Ezra was reading meant (Neh 8:8). Ezra and the Levites were really serving in the ministry of the exegetical escort, for they were escorting the people into the presence of God through the Word of God. The result was that they were transformed, for they began to weep when they heard God's Word and saw themselves in the mirror of God's law, recognizing that they had failed to comply with the demands of the divine (Neh 8:9). They left the worship service transformed; for they ate, drank, shared their food with those who had nothing to eat and proceeded to keep the required Feast of Booths, which they had not celebrated since they were uprooted from their homeland of Jerusalem by Nebuchadnezzar and the Babylonians.

During the intertestamental period of four hundred years, God, who had not spoken through a prophet since Malachi, opened the prophetical scroll and spoke through John the Baptist. John, who would serve as the precursor and public relations manager of Jesus, came on the scene as an exegetical escort and pointed the Jews to Jesus the Messiah, saying, "Behold the Lamb of God, which taketh away the sin of the world" (John 1:29). John the Baptist was so effective in the use of the Old Testament Scriptures, which amplified the person of Christ and the coming of the Messiah, that a large group of Jews around Jerusalem and in all Judea were escorted by the preaching of John and went to the Jordan River, confessed their sins, were baptized by John the Baptist, and experienced transformation.

Andrew, one of John the Baptist's disciples, heard John talk about Jesus and became a follower of the Christ. The first action that Andrew took after becoming a disciple of Jesus was to find his brother Peter and literally to escort him to the presence of the Son of God based upon the authentic proclamation about Him from John as well as his own personal testimony of One whom he now called the Messiah. Peter would also experience transformation, for Jesus would call him by his present name, Simon, and assure him that one day he would be called Cephas, meaning "a rock" (John 1:41–42).

The once-cowardly Peter, who denied his Lord three times, was emboldened as he stood before the Jewish gathering during the Pentecostal feast and proclaimed that Jesus was the Messiah, basing his promulgation on Old Testament texts found in the book of Psalms and the book of Joel. He argued that this Jesus, by the predeterminate counsel of God, was delivered into the hands of Jewish rulers and crucified by the will of the Jewish people. His exegetical escorting of the Jewish hearers by the Word of God into the presence of God was so effective that the Jews, who were convicted of their sin of rejecting the Son of God, asked, "What shall we do?" Peter gave them directions from Scripture. About three thousand of them complied with the directions and were transformed, baptized, and added to the church (Acts 2:41).

An Ethiopian eunuch was returning home from the extended Pentecostal feast in Jerusalem. He was a resident in Ethiopia and held the lofty title of treasurer of Candace, the queen of Ethiopia. Apparently he was greatly affected by the spiritual fervor of the Pentecostal experience, but he was not one of the three thousand persons who had responded to the proclamation of the gospel. Still, the afterglow of the encounter was influencing him, for he was reading the scroll of the prophet Isaiah. The Lord sent an angel to tell Philip to close his ministry in Samaria and go to the Gaza Strip to minister to this sole traveler. Philip came to the eunuch's chariot and asked him if he understood what he was reading. The eunuch was in need of an exegetical escort, for he replied, "How can I unless someone guides me?" Philip proceeded to start at the same place where the eunuch was reading Isaiah 53, and he preached Jesus to the eunuch. He escorted him to the living Lord by showing him that the lamb that was led to the slaughter for some blood, and the sheep that was led to the shearers for some wool, represented Jesus Christ, the Son of God. The two metaphors in Isaiah were conveying the truth of Christ's *cleansing* us by His blood and *covering* us by His righteousness. Upon understanding the truth of the Isaiah 53 text and seeing Christ and His provision for salvation in light of this text, this man believed, experienced transformation, and immediately requested baptism (Acts 8:26–39). After Philip, the exegetical escort, had finished his escorting assignment, he immediately disappeared; for the task of the exegetical escort is to equip the new believer without becoming an enabler for the new believer.

The Jewish married couple, Aquila and Priscilla, became acquainted with Paul the apostle in Corinth after they and other Jewish people had been expelled from Rome by an edict from Emperor Claudius. Through their tent-making trade they met Paul, another tent maker. They served as charter members of the Corinthian church that was founded by Paul. Remaining with Paul for eighteen months in establishing and organizing the Corinthian church, they sailed with Paul to Ephesus, where they would be responsible for the work in the exterior of Ephesus, while Paul went to preach in the synagogue in the interior of Ephesus. During this ministry they heard Apollos speak. He was a native from Alexandria who was eloquent in speech and mighty in the Scriptures, but his biblical message was limited, for he was only acquainted with the message of repentance voiced in the preaching of John the Baptist. Aquila and Priscilla escorted him to their home and, through the Scriptures, gave him a more thorough knowledge of God's Word and apparently demonstrated how the Scriptures related to Jesus. Consequently, Apollos benefited from their exegetical escorting ministry and experienced transformation in his ministry, for he persuasively convinced the Jews of the witness of the Scriptures, showing them that Jesus was the Christ (Acts 18:24–28).

A Brief Look at Eisegetical Escorting

Exegetical escorting is a dynamic in which the preacher, through the proper use and interpretation of the Scriptures, ushers the hearers into the presence of God for the purpose of transformation. Eisegetical escorting is the opposite. Through the misuse and misinterpretation of the Scriptures, the hearers are misled and escorted away from the presence and the intention of God and never experience transformation. Exegesis is the drawing out of the text the author's original meaning within the text. Eisegesis is the putting into the text an interpretation or meaning that is foreign to the text.

Job, the suffering servant of God, experienced a total reversal in his world within a short period of time. He lost children, health, and wealth. Three of his friends, whom he would later refer to as "miserable comforters," heard about his recent disaster and came to comfort him. These men, Eliphaz, Bildad and Zophar, came to the vicinity of Job's residence and did not recognize him from a distance because he was covered with sores all over his body and had been sitting on the ash heap scraping dead flesh from his skin. They began to weep and tear their garments, sprinkling dust on their heads as a sign of mutual mourning for Job. Then, like Ezekiel, they assumed a posture of silence for seven days (Ezek 3:15; Job 2:13) and did not speak a word to him for a whole week. Their ministry of silence was their most valuable gift to Job; but after they had declared a moratorium on speech for seven days, they opened their mouths and, without divine approval, spoke for God. They attributed the recent crises in Job's life to sins he had committed and urged him to repent in order to gain the favor of God and to avert future judgment from God. The closing chapter of the book of Job features God reprimanding these three men for being eisegetical escorts. God was angry with them and said, "Ye have not spoken of me the thing which is right, like my servant Job" (Job 42:8).

Hananiah was an antagonist to Jeremiah. Both were prophets. Jeremiah was a prophet of God; Hananiah was a false prophet. Jeremiah was an exegetical escort who ushered the people of Judah into the presence of God by informing them that the Word of God not only guaranteed their seventy-year captivity but also assured them of a remnant of their nation that would return to Jerusalem and rebuild their civilization. Jeremiah told the citizens of Jerusalem to surrender to the ultimatum of King Nebuchadnezzar of Babylon in order to prevent widespread loss and bloodshed and to prepare to make the best of life in the foreign country of Babylon by building houses, planting gardens, and raising families until the time of their release from captivity and return to their land for restoration. To illustrate this truth of God's Word, Jeremiah provided a visual aid. He put a wooden yoke around his neck and walked through the streets of the city, declaring that God had put a yoke of Babylonian captivity around the neck of the nation of Judah and would allow them to go into captivity to the Babylonians for seventy years. Hananiah broke the wooden yoke and changed the original meaning of that symbol to suit his interests and the desires of the people. In his words the broken yoke represented that within two years God would break the yoke and hold that Nebuchadnezzar had on the nation of Judah. Later God would instruct Jeremiah to put an unbreakable iron yoke around his neck as a symbol that God's Word must be fulfilled and that Judah would go into captivity by the hands of the Babylonians. The Word of the Lord came to pass through His prophet Jeremiah, who escorted the nation into the presence of God even though he was rejected by prophets, priests, kings, and the people. Jeremiah was an exegetical escort who knew that he was not responsible for the transformation of the people. They had the option of receiving or rejecting the word delivered by Jeremiah. On the other hand, Hananiah was an eisegetical escort; for he perverted the truth of God and made it mean what he wanted it to mean. He led the people astray and prevented them from instantly experiencing the transformation of inner tranquility that comes as a result of trusting the Word of God without adjusting the Word of God. Jeremiah informed Hananiah that the Lord had not sent him and indicted him for causing the people to trust in a lie. The wrath of God fell upon Hananiah, and he died the same year of his eisegetical escorting (Jer 28:15–17).

DOCTRINE *That* DANCES

Jesus as an Exegetical Escort

Luke 24:13–36 provides a model for the preacher as an exegetical escort. Jesus, the quintessential exegetical escort, walks with two disciples on the road to Emmaus, escorts them into the presence of God through the expounding of the Word, and they experience a transformation and return to the Eleven with the news of Jesus' resurrection. Jesus initiated them into the faith, instructed them in the faith, and inspired them to keep the faith. Look how the great exegetical escort does this in Luke 24:13–36. On the calendar it is Sunday evening, but in the heart of the two disciples on the Emmaus road, it is Friday afternoon. They are living in the evening of the resurrection, but their minds are on the evening of the crucifixion. They leave Jerusalem. They wanted to get away from the teeming crowds that had gathered there for the Passover. They are a disillusioned, defeated, and frustrated fellowship. They commune together. They walk and talk. They could have gone to Mount Ephraim in the north, but it was probably too far; east to Jericho, but the Jericho road was probably too dangerous; south to Bethlehem, but it would probably remind them of the crib, which in turn would cause them to think about the cross, both of which are the same wood. So they left Jerusalem and went west to a little town named Emmaus. As they are talking and comparing notes, one who had been familiar before the crucifixion becomes strange. He asked them: What is it that you are communing about? Why are your faces so sad? What is the problem? These two men looked at Jesus as a stranger. They did not expect to see Jesus. They respond: Are you just a stranger in these parts? Do you not know what happened outside the walls of Jerusalem last Friday?

To advance the frame two thousand years, it was if they were asking, "Don't you know what happened in New York City on September 11, 2001; Oklahoma City on April 19, 1995; or Pearl Harbor on December 7, 1941?"

Jesus could simply save them fourteen miles of frustration, introspection, and investigation (seven miles from Jerusalem to

Emmaus and a return trip back to Jerusalem) by fast-forwarding to verse 36, "Peace be unto you—I am he!" But Jesus does not immediately expose the truth. He does not give instant and quick answers. He lets them struggle with the question. Jesus is the only One who really knows what is going on, and yet He acts as if He is unaware of recent devastating events. He wants these two men to discover the truth for themselves. He does not want them to be ventriloquists or parrots of the truth they simply hear from others. He wants them not only to know what they believe and why they believe but also who they believe, for they will put their lives on the line for preaching the truth of the resurrection. He wants them to know these pertinent realities so that when He ascends and sits on His throne, the truth will still abide in their hearts.

When we preach to people, we are to preach in such a way that we make ourselves unnecessary. We need to equip them so that they can survive and thrive during a crisis even when we are not accessible to them.

Jesus decides to act as if He were unaware of recent community developments. He did not say that He does not know. He simply asks, "What things?" They inform Him that three days earlier, Jesus, a "prophet mighty in word and in deed," was crucified. And a few women came in their presence and told them that they went to the tomb and found it empty. Two disciples, Peter and John, ran to the tomb and also reported that the tomb was empty. After three days the disciples had given up all hope that He would rise from the dead and become their deliverer from Roman domination. They consider His death final. They think He was the Messiah, but how can you have a dead Messiah?

Jesus was listening, and when He could take no more of their unbelief, He reprimanded them: "O fools, and slow of heart to believe all that the prophets have spoken" (v. 25). He did not call them fools because they did not believe the reports of the women or Peter and John. He called them fools because they did not believe what the Scriptures had said and the promise He made to the disciples to rise from the dead after three days.

Then Jesus asked, "Ought not the Christ to have suffered these things, and to enter into his glory?" (v. 26). This is the theology of the cross and the theology of glory. It is always the cross that precedes the resurrection. Starting with Moses and going through to the prophets, He showed how everything that was written in the Law, the Prophets, and the Writings was written in relation to Him. The Bible is a "Himbook"—it is about Him. He must have explained various texts in the Old Testament that referred to him: "The sceptre shall not depart from Judah, nor a lawgiver from between his feet, until Shiloh come" (Gen 49:10); "A fountain will be opened . . . to cleanse them from sin and impurity" (Zech 13:1 NIV); and "For unto us a child is born, unto us a son is given" (Isa 9:6). He just kept going through the Scriptures, showing them how the Old Testament referred to Him. After a while, they came to the village of Emmaus. Notice that the Greek word for "expound" is *diermeneusen*, which means "to translate," "interpret," or "explain." There Jesus expounded unto them all that was in Scripture that referred to Him (v. 27). This expansion is based on what happened in preexistent eternity. Jesus was able to expound, translate, interpret, and explain the Word of God based on His ability to interpret God. This dynamic is at work in John 1:18: "No one has ever seen God, but God the One and Only, who is at the Father's side, has made him known" (NIV). The Greek word for "declare" is *exegesato*, which means that He, the Son, made the Father known. He explained Him, told of Him, and translated Him. Since He could interpret the Father, He was able to interpret the Scriptures for the disciples because He knew the author. What the author wrote, He could explain to those who were reading the book. So He is explaining Scriptures as an escort. He escorted them to the truth and the promises of the Father so that they could be transformed in their thinking and demeanor. Downcast disciples cannot effectively testify the goodness of the gospel. They have come to the village of Emmaus. They asked Jesus to spend the night with them. Jesus, the exegetical escort, will eventually leave but not until they have been in the shared presence of God in a moment of worship during which he is revealed in the breaking of the bread. The exegetical escort must resist being a necessary presence and leave them in the presence of God, where their perspective and minds are transformed. Jesus, who was guest, became host, and He who was stranger became familiar because in the breaking of bread they recognized him. When? How? Maybe they saw the nail prints in His hands when He lifted up the bread to break and to bless. Maybe the outer garment exposed the gash in His side when He raised His arms. Then He disappeared out of their sight. They had been exegetically escorted.

They began to compare notes: "Did not our heart burn within us, while he talked with us by the way . . . and opened to us the scriptures?" (v. 32). Three things took place: First, there was learning. Their eyes were opened to Scriptures. Second, there was burning: "Did not our hearts burn within us?" Were not our bosoms on fire? Their bosoms were on fire as a result of the encounter with Jesus, who came from the bosom of the Father. The One who came from the bosom of the Father taught them until their bosoms were on fire. Third, there was yearning. They left and went and told the Eleven that the Lord had indeed risen.

They got up that night and traveled across the same seven miles but with a different attitude. No longer was it Good Friday in their thinking. It was literally Resurrection Sunday in their spirits. They told the Eleven what they had seen on the road and how the Lord had made himself visible or known (vv. 34–35). The Greek word for "told" in verse 35 is *exegounto*. It means "related." It is synonymous with the word *diermeneusen* "explained" in verse 27. They exegeted to the Eleven what Jesus had exegeted to them on the road from Jerusalem to Emmaus. So they are following his exegetical escorting example. They did not say anything that

101

they had not heard Him say. Their exegesis matched His exegesis. Their interpretation matched His interpretation. When their exegesis matched His exegesis, verse 36 says that while they were talking the Lord *showed up*. We cannot expect God to *show up* when our exegesis does not match His exegesis. This is eisegesis, or the putting into the text what is not in the text.

Zacharias lacked the faith that he and his wife, Elizabeth, would have a baby in their old age. While Zacharias was performing his priestly duties, the angel Gabriel reported what God had given to him: Gabriel exegeted God's Word to Zacharias. He told him that his aged wife Elizabeth was going to have a son. Zacharias did not believe it. The angel informed him that he was not going to be able to speak until the child was born. Zacharias could not speak for at least nine months. On the day of the circumcision ceremony, which took place on the eighth day after the birth of a Jewish male baby, some of the attendees asked Zacharias what his son would be named. They probably thought that it was going to be Bar-Zacharias (son of Zacharias) or some other great biblical name. Zacharias motioned for a tablet and wrote, "His name is John." Immediately his tongue was loosed, and he wrote the Benedictus and praised God. If he had written any other name, he probably would not have spoken because he would not have said what God had said. If we want power in our preaching, we must make sure that we say what God says. God will *show up* when our exegesis matches His exegesis, and we will see transformation in our ministry.

> I love to tell the story of unseen things above,
> Of Jesus and His glory, of Jesus and His love.
> I love to tell the story, because I know 'tis true;
> It satisfies my longings as nothing else can do.
> I love to tell the story, 'twill be my theme in glory,
> To tell the old, old story of Jesus and His love.[17]

17 A. Katherine Hankey, "I Love to Tell the Story," 1866.

Chapter Five

THE PREACHER AS A DOXOLOGICAL DANCER

Preaching is best done when preachers seek to praise God through their sermon. Praise ought to be the natural response of preachers during the ministry event. Exuberance during the ministry moment should be natural as His Word is declared and heard. Enthusiasm exudes through the pores of the minister's spiritual being. The hearers can sense that the preacher is offering praise to God on behalf of His grace and for the privilege of sharing in the ministry of proclamation.

There is a spirit of insipid intellectualism that is pervading the atmosphere of the church. It is antithetical to freedom of expression in preaching, teaching, and worship. This temperament is liturgically bland and flavorless; it lacks the seasoning of the Spirit of God. Preachers who enter the sanctuary with an insipid attitude toward communicating the Word of God present it in a boring manner. The intellect is significant and must not be left in the vestibule of the church as the preacher prepares to deliver a message from the Lord. While the mind must always be cultivated, the church must be aware of the insipid intellectualism that lacks joy and excludes the Spirit. Dr. D. Martyn Lloyd-Jones, celebrated pastor at Westminster Chapel in London, England, believed that:

> Preaching should be always under the Spirit—His power and control—and yet you do not know what is going to happen, so always be free. It may sound contradictory to say "prepare and prepare carefully," and yet "be free." . . . You will find that the Spirit who has helped you in your preparation may now help you, while you are speaking, in an entirely new way,

and open things out to you which you had not seen while you were preparing your sermon.[1]

There is the prolonged idea in preaching that we simply speak to people from the neck up. These people feel that to be expressive and enthusiastic is to stand on the edge of contrivance, calling attention to oneself. Consequently, some seminaries train their theological students to maintain their emotional composure.

Since God created humans, should not that realm of the human construct be allowed to participate in the sending and receiving of the Word of God? John Wesley was once asked why so many people came to hear him preach. His response was, "When you set yourself on fire, people love to come and see you burn."[2] Preaching must be doxological and not boring.

The Inseparables of Preaching

Didasko is a New Testament word used for teaching or instruction. *Didasko* is content oriented. Similarly, *kerusso* is the New Testament word for preaching. *Kerusso* is intent oriented. *Didasko* and *kerusso* must always be integrated in preaching and teaching. Preaching must always have a function; it must have a clear focus on what it seeks to accomplish. The goal of proclamation is to instruct and invite hearers to salvation, while the purpose of teaching is to instruct believers toward experiencing maturity in discipleship. The objective of therapy is to inspire the mature believer and others to keep the faith in spite of the loss of relationship, health, and wealth. The heart and mind must remain in tension so that the will of the Christian to keep the faith in the midst of crises is never relinquished.

Epistemology is the study of truth. Ontology is focused on the study of being human. Both have to remain together. After the

1 D. Martyn Lloyd-Jones, *Preaching and Preachers* (Grand Rapids: Zondervan, 1972), 85.
2 John Wesley, http://www.giga-usa.com/quotes/authors/john_wesley_a001.htm.

preacher answers the "what" question of epistemology, the hearers await the fulfillment of the "so what" and "now what" questions of ontology. They want to know the difference truth makes in their human circumstances. Does the sermon make a difference when the hearers have to go back to jobs they despise or to houses without love? Does the sermon make a difference when they have to face possible surgery? What difference is epistemology, or truth, going to make in the ontological circumstances of their human condition?

May I Have This Dance?

While the escort metaphor is fresh and new to homiletical literature, the dancing metaphor has been widely employed by prominent homileticians, theologians, popular writers, contemporary music artists, and television producers. The dancing metaphor is featured in the title of Eugene Lowry's homiletical text, *Dancing the Edge of Mystery.*[3] Other books from various fields that include the dancing metaphor in their titles are Henri Nouwen's contemplative work *Turn My Mourning into Dancing,*[4] Elaine Moise's Jewish Passover manual *The Dancing with Miriam Haggadah: A Jewish Women's Celebration of Passover,*[5] Ray Buckley's *Dancing with Words,*[6] William Frey's *The Dance of Hope,*[7] William Easum's *Dancing with Dinosaurs: Ministry in a Hostile and Hurting World,*[8]

3 Eugene Lowry, *The Sermon: Dancing the Edge of Mystery* (Nashville: Abingdon, 1997).
4 Henri Nouwen, *Turn My Mourning into Dancing* (Nashville: Thomas Nelson, 2004).
5 Elaine Moise, *The Dancing with Miriam Haggadah: A Jewish Women's Celebration of Passover* (Mountain View, CA: Rikudei Miriam, 1997).
6 Ray Buckley, *Dancing with Words: Storytelling as Legacy, Culture, and Faith* (Nashville: Discipleship Resources, 2004).
7 William Frey, *The Dance of Hope: Finding Ourselves in the Rhythm of God's Great Story* (Colorado Springs: WaterBrook, 2003).
8 William Easum, *Dancing with Dinosaurs: Ministry in a Hostile and Hurting World* (Nashville: Abingdon, 1993).

and Sam Keen's *To a Dancing God*.[9] And of course, Hollywood has always embraced the dancing metaphor. Examples of this are *Dirty Dancing*[10] starring Patrick Swayze, *Shall We Dance*[11] featuring Richard Gere and Jennifer Lopez, and *Dancing with the Stars*,[12] showcasing movie and television stars who learn how to dance from professional dancers. Music and dance have always been integrally related to each other. Donna Summer's "Last Dance"[13] and the classical rendition "I Could Have Danced All Night"[14] are memorable musical pieces. Even "The Lord of the Dance," which was written over four hundred years ago, demonstrates that the dance metaphor has been in vogue for a long time.

As previously noted, with regard to "exegetical escort," the word *exegetical* is acceptable without any question because it relates to biblical interpretation. However, *escort* carries with it a sinister semantic and needs sacred sanitizing because of the initial immoral connotations of the word. With the "doxological dance," *doxological* is acceptable without suspicion because it refers to the praise of God (*doxa* means "praise"). *Dance*, however, like *escort*, also has a sinister semantic and is stained in the eyes of many churches. Some churches have considered dancing to be a worldly or secular activity, having no role to play in sacred employment. The exegetical and the doxological serve as counselors who counsel the escort and dance metaphors. Thus, both metaphors are emptied of their sinister semantic. The escort metaphor is filled with exegetical liquid, and the dance metaphor is filled with doxological fluid. The escort and the dance become inseparably linked in the preaching event.

9 Sam Keen, *To a Dancing God* (New York: Harper & Row, 1970).
10 *Dirty Dancing*, dir. Emile Ardolino, perf. Patrick Swayze and Jennifer Grey, VHS, Vestron, 1987.
11 *Shall We Dance*, dir. Peter Chelsom, perf. Richard Gere and Jennifer Lopez, DVD, Miramax Films, 2004.
12 *Dancing with the Stars*, ABC, USA, 2007 season.
13 Donna Summer's, "Last Dance," 1978.
14 "I Could Have Danced All Night," from *My Fair Lady*, Alan Jay Lerner and Frederick Lowe, 1956.

The Doxological Dancer

In the song "I Hope You Dance," popular music artist LeAnn Womack sings, "If you have the chance to sit it out or dance, I hope you'll dance. Dance like no one is watching and love like you'll never get hurt."[15] *The purpose of the preacher as a doxological dancer is to communicate the doctrinal message of the Bible with accuracy and ardor so that the exuberant hearer exults in the exaltation of God.* Using the Word, preachers as exegetical escorts usher the hearers to the throne room of God to encounter God's presence. While the preacher escorts the hearers through the substance of the Word of God, the preachers also doxologically dance with exuberance, having themselves already been in God's presence.

The preachers are simultaneously exegetical escorts and doxological dancers as they respond respectively to the substance of the Word of God within a style that is unique to their own personality yet reflective of an enthusiastic and passionate delivery. Doctrinal preaching includes both the exegetical escorting of the hearer and the doxological dancing of the preacher as the preacher ushers the hearer into the presence of God for the purpose of transformation. The preacher, who prior to the preaching moment has been transformed and who dances in the delivery of the message, expects the hearers also to be doxologically responsive to the Word of God because of the transformative moment. The doxological response in the preaching and hearing of the Word of God does not enter the sermon in its conclusion; rather, it begins the sermon in its introduction and resounds throughout the message.

Doxology is the alpha and omega of the alphabet of preaching. The doxological dance is part of the experience. The doctrinal message of the Bible must be *preaching*. It is not a dynamic that is employed in order to get to the conclusion! The preacher is taking the people on a trip and enjoying the journey as well. Preaching is

---

15 Mark Daniel Sanders and Tia Sillers, "I Hope You Dance," 2000. Permission granted.

107

not a monological event; it is a dialogical exercise. The preacher preaches so that the church may preach.

Phillips Brooks's classic definition of preaching embodies the purpose of the preacher as a doxological dancer: "Preaching is the communication of truth by man to men."[16] It is actualized in a veritable homiletical ping-pong dynamic. The preacher serves the sermon to the congregation, and the congregation serves the sermon back to the preacher. This exchange may be in the form of nonverbal "feel back" and verbal "talk back," known as "call and response" in the African American preaching experience. Information and inspiration are inextricably intertwined. This twofold witness in preaching produces exuberance in the hearer, who responds to it with exultation and joy and fulfills the goal of all preaching in exalting and giving glory to God!

What is the difference between *exult* and *exalt?* Exultation, or rejoicing in God, leads to the exalting or the lifting up of God for humanity to see. It is important that both the preacher and the hearer rejoice in God so that God may be lifted up in praise. John Piper asserts, "God is most glorified when we are most satisfied in Him."[17] The ultimate objective in preaching is the exaltation of God. Jesus tells us, "And I, when I am lifted up from the earth, will draw all people to myself" (John 12:32 ESV). Exultation in preaching is not determined by any prerequisite emotional experience prior to the preaching moment. Exultation is predicated on the preacher being encountered by the Lord. If the preacher exults in the Lord in the prayer room and study, the channels will be open for the preacher to motivate the hearers to mutually participate in the exaltation of God in the pulpit. The internal preacher's dialogue with the Lord in private serves as a catalyst for an external enterprise of giving glory to God and exalting the most high God.

16 Phillips Brooks, *Lectures on Preaching* (New York: Dutton, 1877), 5.
17 John Piper, http://expositorythoughts.wordpress.com/2007/04/28/lunch-meeting-with-john-piper/, accessed May 16, 2007.

The Westminster Shorter Catechism is commonly interpreted as saying, "The duty of man is to glorify God and enjoy Him forever." Happiness is not an ingredient of the fruit of the Spirit; joy is! Joy transcends happiness. One can be happy as long as happy things are happening! Joy is like the stone chimney that remains standing alone after the wooden house in the country has been reduced to rubble and ashes by fire. Preaching exults in God, and the exultation is designed to establish the exaltation in the hearts of the congregation as the people hear the Word of God from the lips of a preacher who is enthusiastic, excited, and having fun in the pulpit! How can a preacher who opposes exultation motivate people to exalt the God who is the epitome and the express image of joy?

Preaching and theology exist for praise or doxology. Theology may serve as a monitor of conscience for preaching, and preaching may serve as a monitor of conscience for theology. The Spirit of God moves within the preacher as the preacher interacts with the Word. Joy in preaching is contagious. "Let the redeemed of the LORD say so" (Ps 107:2).

Nobel Peace Prize winner Elie Wiesel, a German who is a survivor of the Holocaust, pictured rabbis who loved the Torah as crawling into the cranium of Yahweh. The crawling into the cranium of God is not just a cognitive activity dealing with the mind but also an affective engagement relating to the heart and its emotions. The word *yadah* means "to know." It is not just to know cognitively but affectively and experientially. *Yadah* is not just a head relationship; it is also a heart relationship. It is both cranial and cardiological. Hosea 4:6 asserts, "My people are destroyed for a lack of knowledge." The word in this text for knowledge is *yahdah*. Cranial and cardiological. They knew the Law in their head, but relationally speaking, their hearts were divorced from the One who gave the Law. Preaching is both crawling into the cranium of God to acquire the Word of God and crawling out of the cranium of God to deliver the message with fervor and conviction because of the preacher's being in an intimate relationship with God.

Many theologies are often right in what they affirm but wrong in what they deny. Many sermons are not getting a congregational hearing not because of their lack of substance but because of a deficit that lacks the demonstration of the Spirit and the holistic involvement of preacher to people—body, mind, and spirit.

The influence of the Greco-Roman mind-set influenced the preaching of the ancient church after the first century. Increasing emphasis was geared toward the mind and knowledge; the heart and emotions were de-emphasized. John the apostle dealt with the doctrine of docetism in his first epistle. This doctrine, espoused by the Gnostics, denied that Jesus had a physical body because flesh is evil. In their thinking, for God in Christ to be incarnated and to take on flesh would mean that God in Christ would become contaminated, dressed in a garment of physiological evil, thus disqualifying Him for salvific service. In response to this increasingly prevalent heresy, John wrote, "Every spirit that confesses that Jesus Christ has come in the flesh is from God, and every spirit that does not confess Jesus is not from God" (1 John 4:2–3 ESV).

Another drawback of this heresy was its de-emphasis and, in some instances, the exclusion of emotion which, of course, was activated through the human body. Emotions were rendered suspect. At best, personal discipline was called upon to keep one's emotions in check. Cultivating the mind was the most significant pursuit. This war between the cranial (mind and understanding) and the cardiological (heart and emotions) continued for twenty centuries and is still an important issue in preaching in the twenty-first century.

The previously mentioned seventeenth-century philosopher, René Descartes, constructed his famous dictum: *Cogito ergo sum* (I think, therefore I am). He was a product of the Enlightenment. His dictum encouraged measuring reality on the basis of the knowledge of the mind. Emotions were ruled out as a reliable and trustworthy instrument for measuring reality. Even in the seventeenth-century, emotions were suspect. People were instructed to believe that they were what they were because of their minds and what they thought. In some circles preaching tended to be "from the neck up."

The Pentecostal movement began in Los Angeles in 1906 during the Azusa Street revival. It was a response to the Enlightenment's attempt to keep the lid on emotions. In response to René Descartes's dictum, Pentecostalism's dictum would in some respect be, "Sensuo ergo sum," (I feel, therefore I am). As the Enlightenment's emphasis had been on the head, Pentecostalism's emphasis was on the heart; and the trajectory, in some measure, was from the neck down. This movement tended to be "big-hearted," whereas in the Enlightenment period there was the tendency toward "big-headedness." Pentecostalism's counsel was not to trust anything outside of the Spirit. Promising young preachers were oftentimes counseled against attending Bible college or seminary because the Spirit and the Word were considered enough for equipping their future ministers and pastors. It was feared that the Pentecostal member who attended a Bible college or theological seminary would return to the Pentecostal church with a full head of information but would lose the fire of the Spirit that brought inspiration in preaching.

To preach only to the heads of people puts one in the category of a "big-headed preacher." A preacher who excludes the heads of the congregation and totally focuses on the congregation's heart is a "beheaded preacher." Preaching must have a bifocal trajectory: it must focus on both head and heart. It is not an either/or proposition but a both/and implementation. Jesus said, "Love the Lord thy God with all thy heart, and with all thy soul, and with all thy mind" (Matt 22:37). Preaching must inform and inspire; it must be holistic in nature. Preaching is right in affirming that the sermon's content is crucial to its effectiveness but incorrect in denying the freedom of emotional experience in its process. God the Creator, who made human beings in the image of the Creator, is passionate. Shouldn't preachers who are stamped within the fabric of their beings with the signature of the Sovereign One reflect the mind of God (thought) and the spirit of God (emotions)? Holistic preaching must be directed to holistic hearers who are both cognitive (mind) and affective (emotions) in responding to the message of the preacher.

The Style of Doctrinal Preaching

If the exegetical escort relates to the substance of preaching while the doxological dancer addresses the style of preaching, then what is the matter with the style of doctrinal preaching? There is an imbalance between its substance and its style. One of the darkest moments in Jewish history is portrayed in Judges 2:10 (ESV): "After that whole generation had been gathered to their ancestors, another generation grew up who knew neither the LORD nor what he had done for Israel." The conversation between Augustine's work, *De Doctrina Christiana* (On Christian Doctrine), written in the fifth century, and François Fénelon's work, *Dialogues on Eloquence*, written in the seventeenth century, must be revisited for the sake of maintaining the proper balance in preaching. Augustine's treatise is devoted to four books: the first three books treat the substance of preaching (hermeneutics), and the fourth and final book treats the style of preaching (homiletics). So three-fourths of Augustine's work emphasizes the substance of preaching, and one-fourth addresses the style of preaching. Style or delivery is not ignored; it is assigned its proper role and place. Augustine emphasized substance over style, and twelve centuries after Augustine, Fenelon recognized that a significant portion of his congregants were uninformed about basic Christian teaching. Convinced that the spiritual health and vitality of the church needed to be founded upon the truths of Scripture, Fenelon closes *Dialogues on Eloquence* with a quote from Saint Jerome:

When you teach in the church, do not stir up applause; stir up lamentations in the people. Let the tears of your listeners be your praise. The discourses of a preacher must be full of sacred Scripture. Don't be a declaimer, but a true teacher of the mysteries of your God.[18]

Twenty-first-century preachers must be intentional about delivering sermons that are substantive without ignoring the significance of style.

Reversal of the Canons of Criticism

What is the matter with the style of doctrinal preaching? *There is a reversal of the Greco-Roman five canons of criticism.* The fifth canon, delivery, appears to have taken priority over the first canon, invention, in contemporary preaching. The first three canons are from the Greeks, and the last two are from the Romans. The first canon, *invention*, relates to the gathering of substance, or the material for the speech act; the second, *arrangement*, deals with the arrangement of the substance; the third treats *style*, or the word or phrase selection; the fourth canon addresses *memory*; and the fifth canon looks at the dynamic of *delivery*. If we want people to be persuaded by what we are preaching, we must first be persuaded ourselves. Conviction is contagious.

Under *invention*, the first canon, Aristotle says that three available means are used to persuade people. He calls them modes of proof. The first mode of proof is *ethos*. This is the integrity, credibility, or character of the preacher. For Aristotle, *ethos* is the perceived character of a good man speaking well. For the serious-minded preacher, homiletics in its truest sense is not merely the preparation and delivery of the sermon: it is also the preparation and delivery of the preachers themselves. The second mode of proof is *pathos*. This is the emotive and passionate sector of the preacher. Jeremiah 20:9

18 Francois de Salignac de la Mothe Fenelon, *Dialogues on Eloquence*, trans. Wilbur Samuel Howell (Princeton, NJ: Princeton University Press, 1951), 153.

20:9 provides a great example of passion for preaching: "His word was in mine heart as a burning fire shut up in my bones." Passion is the external expression of the preacher as the truth of Scripture is illumined in the mind of the preacher. The third mode of proof is *logos*. This is the gathering of content and material for the sermon. How can one be credibly passionate without *logos*? Passion is released when the preacher is engaged by the text. An empty wagon makes a lot of noise. So invention primarily relates to the materials that are gathered for our sermons. In other words: *preparation*.

The second canon is the *arrangement* of the material. The material has to be arranged so that it flows logically and is interesting. Arrangement is important. Haddon Robinson wrote in his diary about preaching, "[Harry Ironside] preached for an hour and it seemed like twenty minutes; others preach for twenty minutes and it seems like an hour. I wonder what the difference is?" The rest of his life was dedicated to answering this question.[19] George Bernard Shaw got up to speak and apologized for the length of his message. He said that it would have been shorter if he had had more time. Shaw was acknowledging that if he had more time, he would have squeezed the speech until the unnecessary and extraneous elements were extracted. Preachers of the Word must make every word count because people do not come to church to waste time.

The third canon is *style*. This canon has to do with the words we use in our preaching. There is the right word and the almost right word. Mark Twain said, "The difference between the right word and the almost right word is a large matter—it's the difference between the lightning bug and the lightning."[20] The lightning has power! Preachers need to pray over their words and select

---

19 Haddon Robinson, *Making a Difference in Preaching* (Grand Rapids: Baker, 1999), 11.
20 Mark Twain, in a letter to George Bainton, October 15, 1888.

words that visually and relevantly communicate the biblical inten-tion of their sermons.

The fourth canon is *memory*. Memory is the forgotten canon. Preachers need to trust their minds in their preaching endeavors. It is impossible for the preacher to bring up information to the first floor of articulation when the basement of preparation is bare and empty. The Holy Spirit brings to our remembrance what is in the file system of the mind. However, if nothing has been put in the mind to remember, does the preacher expect the Holy Spirit to create something out of nothing (*creatio ex nihilo*)? If there is nothing in the basement of the mental file cabinet, the first floor of delivery is a disaster! We are told that we maximally use only 10 percent of our mental capacity. This means that 90 percent of our mental capacity remains untapped. Memory is hard work. In the movie *Ray*, Ray Charles, visually challenged, memorized his surroundings by becoming familiar with them. Charles was asked, "How do you know what color of socks you are taking out of the drawer?" He responded, "Brown is four, blue is three, two is white, and black is one."[21] He just became familiar with his socks by feel-ing the number on the sock. He could go into a room and know where to find his aftershave lotion and washcloth. He just famil-iarized himself with it. Preachers ought to move from memorizing to picturizing, internalizing, actualizing, and eventually turning the ink of the manuscript into the blood of their life.

Professional athletic teams generally have three squads—first, second, and third string. All the players are required to attend practice. All of the players are required to dress in uniform for the game. All of the players are required to participate in pregame warmups. Infrequently do players on the second squad get in the game. The players on the third squad get in the game even less than the players on the second squad. But when a player or two from the first squad foul out or get injured, players from the second, or

21 *Ray*, dir. Taylor Hackford, perf. Jaime Foxx, Anvil Films, distributed by Uni-versal Pictures, 2004.

even the third squad will be put in the game and are expected to be competitive because they know the plays and have practiced with the players of the first squad. If the preacher prepares well, there will be thoughts and ideas that were not targeted for use in the sermon. But when intended sermonic thoughts drop out of the mind, the preacher may instantly call upon second- and third-squad thoughts that were not slated to get action in the sermon. The congregation will not be aware of your replacement sermonic thoughts.

Finally, the fifth canon is *delivery*. Effective delivery is based on assimilation, not imitation. Be a honeybee and go from flower to flower and gather pollen to make your own honey. Preachers should appreciate the delivery of other preachers, but they must find their own voice. Paul says in Galatians 2:20, "I am crucified with Christ; and it is no longer I who live, but Christ lives in me" (NASB). This verse may be homiletically rephrased: I am crucified with Christ and therefore I preach, yet not I, but T. D. Jakes preaches in me; yet not I, but Charles Swindoll preaches in me; yet not I, but Adrian Rogers preaches in me; yet not I, but Gardner Taylor preaches in me. When preachers adopt other deliveries and voices in the Sunday pulpit, a time will come when they forget who they are supposed to be and which preaching voice is to be heard on that Sunday. Preachers must find *their own* voice and delivery style so that they can be maximally used in the uniqueness of their own personality through the power of the Holy Spirit.

What is the matter with the style of preaching? Preachers have reversed invention (which has to do primarily with *logos*, or the gathering of the material) with delivery. In effect, they give delivery the nod over preparation. Invention is the first canon and delivery is the fifth canon. One of the most glaringly problematic areas in the style of preaching is that invention, the first canon, as it relates to priority and importance, has been relegated to last; and delivery, the last canon, has been elevated to first. The first has become last. Preachers of the Word must return to invention because preparation is the bridge to effective delivery execution. We must redo the reversal of invention and delivery and place them in their proper priority.

Enhancing Doctrinal Preaching

Doctrinal preaching could be greatly buttressed and supported by employing several practical helps. The first is the use of *theological hymns*, which highlight the doctrine under consideration in the sermon and add poetry and power. The theology would be matched with the hymn and the text. Many hymns teach theology and the Bible very profoundly. Sermonic eschatonics demonstrates the movement, rhythm, and elevation of hymns as they point to the eschaton, or the glory land. Hymns move from earth to heaven, from time to eternity, and from mortality to immortality.

The hymn "Amazing Grace" moves from the terrestrial of "Through many dangers, toils and snares" to the celestial of "When we've been there ten thousand years, bright shining as the sun, we've no less days to sing God's praise than when we'd first begun."[22] Hymns like "How Great Thou Art" and "It Is Well with My Soul" are like Jacob's ladder: they begin on earth and conclude in heaven. Preaching must look at every Scripture passage and ask, "Where is the eschaton in this text?" Preachers would be wise to exegete the text of the Scripture and the text of the song during the course of the sermon. Rhythmically reciting the lyrics of a sound theological hymn that is related to the text is an effective way to conclude the sermon and allows the hearers some sacred space to get in rhythm verbally and nonverbally with the preacher.

The second way that doctrinal preaching can be greatly buttressed and enhanced is through *personal testimony*. People do not just want to know that God brought Daniel out of the lion's den. They want to know if preachers have ever been in the lion's den and experienced God's delivering power. Three times Paul's

22 John Newton, "Amazing Grace," 1772.

testimony about his conversion experience is given in the book of Acts.[23] The tribulation saints overcame persecution by the blood of the Lamb and by their testimony (Rev 12:11). The preacher's testimony must be a servant of the text and never seek to master or take over the text. The testimony will have power when it reinforces the message of the text; it will lose power when it gives a message that is antithetical to the text. God has promised to bless His Word about Himself and not necessarily our words about Him. But the preacher's testimony that is consistent with the interpretation and message of the text will provide encouragement and edification for the congregation. In doing this, preachers must guard against committing ecclesiastical nudity every Sunday, hanging all of the soiled garments of their recent experiences on the line for the congregation to see. People do not necessarily need to "see through you" to know that God has "seen you through." Preachers should avoid embarrassing themselves, their family, and the church. They must be selective about the matters they choose to incorporate into the sermon as a testimony.

The third way in which doctrinal preaching could be greatly buttressed would be if it were more *innovative in its arrangement* and less predictable in its approach. When people know how every message will begin and end, they tend to check out before the benediction. Preachers must be willing to be adaptable in their preaching process without adapting the truth of the message. Sermons ought to stimulate people to discover the truth in the text that is being developed by the preacher and to experience a type of sermonic serendipity as they walk with the preacher throughout the sermon. Jesus was a very innovative preacher who resisted predictability. There were times when He finished His message that the hearers recognized that they were the focus of His indictment and did not discover this truth until Jesus had dismissed the class and they were on their way home.

23 Acts 9; 22; and 26.

One day I caught a glimpse of the movie *The Green Mile*.[24] I really did not have time to watch it. I knew that the movie lasted for more than three hours. I made the mistake of sitting in front of the television for fifteen minutes, and then it was all over! I had to see how this miscarriage of justice was going to end. It was just so arresting and engaging. If a movie that I did not have time to watch in the first place could hold me for three hours, then preachers certainly ought to prepare and present messages that have built-in dramatic movement that can hold the interest of the people for the duration of the sermon without boring them. Jesus captivated the Nazareth attendees of His inaugural message just by reading the assigned passages. Luke records, "And the eyes of all them that were in the synagogue were fastened on him" (Luke 4:20).

A Consideration of Dance in Scripture

German philosopher Friedrich Nietzsche remarked, "I would believe only in a God that knows how to dance."[25] In relation to preaching, dancing is an act of celebration in response to the act of God. It is not predicated on oratory or elocution. It is the natural response of the preacher in relation to the supernatural acts of God evidenced in His Word and manifested in the midst of God's people. Bishop William Frey said in a sermon preached at Beeson Divinity School's Pastors School, "Where the words end, the dance begins."[26] The dance may also be a bodily, nonverbal response to the demonstration of the power of God displayed in His Word and among His people. Apparently, there is a likeness of dancing in heaven, for in creation the morning stars sing together and the sons of God shout for joy (Job 38:7). Sam Keen's

---

24 *The Green Mile*, dir. Frank Darabont, perf. Tom Hanks, Michael Clarke Duncan. Castle Rock Entertainment, 1999.
25 Friedrich Nietzsche, *Thus Spake Zarathustra*, trans. R. J. Hollingdale (New York: Penguin, 1969), 153.
26 Beeson Divinity School's Pastors School, Birmingham, AL, July 2003.

119

book title, *To a Dancing God*, is suggestive of a God who dances.[27] David danced before the Lord (2 Sam 6:14; 1 Chron 15:29). His dancing was in response to the ark of God being returned to Jerusalem. Symbolically speaking, God was returning home. David's wife Michal did not appreciate his dancing even though his motive was to give thanks to God for providing a way for Israel to reclaim the ark. Michal accused David of dancing to impress the young maidens and criticized David for it. The doxological dance is always a response to the mighty acts of God done on behalf of the people of God. David did not hold back his response, for he danced with all his might regardless of the criticism from his wife. Preachers must not be intimidated by critics when they offer their whole selves in the preaching event in response to God's grace. David exhorts the people to dance before the Lord in response to the Lord taking pleasure in His people (Ps 149:3–4) and admonishes the people to praise God with the dance in response to His mighty acts (Ps 150:4). Additionally David exclaims, "You have turned for me my mourning into dancing" (Ps 30:11 ESV). What a motive for celebration!

In the parable of the prodigal son, the prodigal son returns home after squandering his possessions and embarrassing his family. Instead of a rebuke, he received a reception: roasted veal with all the trimmings, dinner guests and family members, music and dancing (Luke 15:25). Dancing was taking place in the reception hall in response to the return of the prodigal son and the goodwill of his father. The elder brother was in the field and heard the music and the dancing. He wondered what was going on: why the dancing? The father informed him of the reclamation of the younger brother who was lost but now was found; was dead, being out of fellowship with his father, but was now alive. So the dancing in the reception hall was in response to the return of the younger son. The dancing was also in response to heaven's will. There is joy in heaven when one sinner repents. Heaven and

27 Sam Keen, *To a Dancing God* (New York: Harper & Row, 1970).

earth dance when sinners come to the Lord! Zephaniah 3:17 is one of the most overlooked texts in the entire Bible; it declares that God rejoices over us with singing. God dances? Angels dance? Heaven dances? Earth ought to be a Kodak moment of what is taking place in heaven. If exuberance and joy dictate the climate of heaven, then they should form the atmosphere of earth. "Thy kingdom come, Thy will be done in earth, as it is in heaven" (Matt 6:10). The preacher who would be a doxological dancer during the preaching event must determine to celebrate even when the "elder brother" refuses to participate in the celebrative dance.

Preachers who assume the posture of the doxological dancer and celebrate during the preaching moment in response to God's mighty acts must not be oblivious of the fact that hearers may be resistant to the biblical message and disinclined to participatory dancing. Jesus is the ultimate example. In a brief depiction of His ministry, Jesus revealed that the Pharisees and the lawyers would not appropriately respond by dancing. Preachers who choose to be doxological dancers in their preaching must make that choice in response to God's mighty acts and not in response to congregational emotionalism or resistance. Doxological dancing must be consistent because God is faithful and consistent. The determination to dance or not to dance must not be based on audience but on the Spirit. In the lyrics of the Negro spiritual, "Ev'ry time I feel the Spirit moving in my heart I will pray."

A Case Study of Doxological Duping

Doxological duping is the act of motivating people to respond in reception to the claims of the preacher instead of responding in celebration to the mighty acts of God. Doxological dancing is the ministry of the Word that motivates people to respond in celebration to the mighty acts of God. To dupe is to trick. To dupe is to pull the wool over another's eye. To dance is to exuberantly respond to the grace of God that has been given to the preacher

121

and people. Doxological duping took place in Exodus 32:19–35. God had called Moses up for a summit meeting on Mount Sinai. He had been there for forty days. The assistant pastor, Aaron, the brother of Moses, had been left in charge. The people were complaining, wondering where Pastor Moses was. Moses had been out of view for over a month. They did not know what happened to Moses, and they thought that he may not come back. So sure enough, the assistant pastor, Aaron, took over the position. They wanted gods who would go before them. Aaron said, "All right, I will take what I learned down in Egypt. Bring me your jewelry: your rings, bracelets, and all of your gold and let me melt it." And when he melted it, he made two golden calves and said, "These are the gods that brought you out of Egypt." Well, how could those calves have brought them out of Egypt when the calves had just come into existence? The people started dancing around the calves (v. 19); it was really a case of doxological duping. They were duped into dancing and proceeded to participate in an orgy. They were naked, and the dance had nothing to do with an activity for the glory of God.

John the Baptist attempted to escort Herod Antipas into the presence of God by using the commandment forbidding adultery (Exod 20:14). Herod had taken his brother Philip's wife and married her. Herodias's daughter, at the command of her mother, danced before King Herod Antipas and his guests and not before the King of kings. Herod Antipas had made a banquet prepared to honor his own birthday, and the daughter of Herodias danced. It was actually the worst case of doxological duping, for the mother requested that John the Baptist's head be cut off.

A Case Study of Doxological Dancing

God had completely destroyed Pharaoh and his hosts and assigned the watery grave of the Red Sea as their place of entombment. Exodus 15:1–21 is a musical medley sung in response to the mighty acts of God done on behalf of God's glory and God's people, whom He had promised to deliver after four hundred years. Moses writes this song of exultation and exaltation to God. This is a God-centered passage. In verse 1 God is both object and subject: "I will sing unto the LORD for He hath triumphed gloriously: the horse and the rider hath He thrown into the sea." Verse 2 gives the rationale for praising God. There is also the image of God as a terrible God, an awesome God, and a man-of-war. Verse 3 extols the God of omnipotence. Verses 4–10 display the attributes of God. God blows with his nostrils, and the waters in the Red Sea divide. Verse 11 amplifies the fact that God is incomparable: "Who shall we liken unto God?" Verses 6 and 12 emphasize the right hand of God—the hand of power. Verses 13–17 articulate how fearful the enemies are because they know that God was fighting for Israel. Verse 18 declares that the Lord reigns. The Hebrew word is *malek*, which means that God keeps succeeding Himself. The reason God succeeds Himself as Lord is that there is no one else to succeed Him. He just keeps on succeeding Himself. He is not voted in. He is not nominated. Let us say, then, that God remains on the throne because He keeps on succeeding Himself. Presidents, kings, and popes are elected and die, but God continues to succeed Himself as King of kings and Lord of lords. When King Uzziah's throne is unoccupied, God is on the throne because he keeps on succeeding Himself.

Miriam, the sister of Moses, participates in the act of exulting in God and exalting God. She sings the same song that Moses and the men had sung, but she dances and the women follow her. There is singing, tambourine playing, and dancing. They danced in response to God's mighty acts of delivering Israel. Thus, it is a doxological dance. Miriam and the women are dancing in response to God's incomparableness, faithfulness, and awesomeness. When we preach, we exegetically escort people into the presence of God for the purpose of transformation while we doxologically dance. Although the exegetical escorting precedes the doxological dancing, both are necessary for effective biblical preaching. Doxological dancing without exegetical escorting leaves the congregation uninformed, and exegetical escorting without doxological dancing leaves the congregation uninspired.

Luke 24:13–36 is the primary interpretive picture of the preacher as the exegetical escort. It also has an implicit picture of the doxological dancer. Two disciples are leaving Jerusalem on Resurrection Sunday, but they are living in a Good Friday world. The devastating effects of Good Friday are still at work in them. As a result, they cannot doxologically dance. There must be at least four elements in place in order to doxologically dance: (1) the right face, (2) the right embrace, (3) the right pace, and (4) the right space. These disciples do not have the *right face*. Their faces are probably downcast, and they stand still, looking sad (Luke 24:17). Doxological dancing requires the *right face*, a face from which confidence exudes. They do not have the *right embrace*. They think Jesus is a stranger (Luke 24:18). One does not generally dance up close and personal in the embrace of a stranger. Slow, up-close, and personal dances are generally not reserved for strangers but for lovers. They think He is a stranger. They do not recognize Him. They are not looking for Him because they think He is dead and buried in Joseph's tomb. A dead man is not expected to appear on the road and ask a question. They were not looking for Him—certainly not in the form of the living, risen, resurrected Christ. They cannot embrace Him; He is a stranger. They do not have the *right pace*. They are walking, but their conversation is demoralizing, and they are sad. Undoubtedly their sad conversation prevents them from having a fast-paced walk. It is difficult to dance with a rapid pace when one is discouraged. Finally, they do not have the *right space*. They are on their way to Emmaus, which is not the place for one to dance. One dances in Jerusalem. That is where Jesus rose. Emmaus is the place one goes to avoid the unavoidable. Emmaus is the place one goes to circumvent the inevitable. Emmaus is where one goes to ignore the ensuing moment of reality. Emmaus is the place one goes to foreclose on the future and to cancel tomorrow. Emmaus is the place people go to drown themselves in their tears. Dancing is reserved for Jerusalem. Dancing will occur in a few hours and in less than fifty days on the day of Pentecost. Dancing is to take place in Jerusalem, the city of the resurrection of Jesus. The two disciples and Jesus finally near Emmaus, a village seven miles from Jerusalem. They invite Jesus to be a guest in their home, and He kindly obliges them. As a guest, He becomes the host. Jesus gives thanks for the bread, takes it, breaks and blesses it, and delivers it to the disciples. They recognize Him in the breaking of the bread.

They experience a major breakthrough after having had a major breakdown in their faith. Now they are ready to dance. They have the *right face*. If their hearts are burning, that is, their bosoms are on fire, it seems reasonable to think that a burning heart will make for a glowing face. They have the *right embrace*, for He is their risen, revealed Lord; and they feel close to the Savior who is not the stranger they thought He was. They have the *right pace*. They go back to Jerusalem that night with lightened hearts and undoubtedly quicker feet. They cannot wait to tell the Eleven the good news. Finally, they have the *right space*. They go to the place where the Eleven are gathered and begin to share the story of what their risen Lord had taught them from the Scriptures on the road and how He had revealed Himself to them in their Emmaus home. They are certainly in the right space, not only because the eleven disciples are there but also because Jesus shows up (v. 36) as they are simultaneously exegetical escorts and doxological dancers for the eleven disciples. And Jesus says to them, "Peace be unto you" (John 20:19 ESV).

Jesus is "Lord of the Dance" in this Sydney Carter hymn:

> I danced in the morning when the world was begun,
> And I danced in the moon and the stars and the
> sun,

And I came down from heaven and I danced on the
   earth,
At Bethlehem I had my birth.

Dance then, wherever you may be:
I am the Lord of the dance, said he,
I'll lead you all wherever you may be;
I'll lead you all in the dance, said he.

I danced on the Sabbath when I cured the lame,
The holy people said it was a shame;
They whipped and they stripped and they hung me
   high;
And they left me there on a cross to die.

I danced on a Friday and the sky turned black;
It's hard to dance with the devil on your back;
They buried my body and they thought I'd gone,
But I am the dance and I still go on.

They cut me down and I leapt up high,
I am the life that'll never, never die;
I'll live in you if you'll live in me;
I am the Lord of the Dance, said he.

I danced for the scribe and the Pharisee,
But they would not dance and they wouldn't follow
   me;
I danced for the fishermen, for James and for John;
They came to me and the dance went on.[28]

28 Sydney Carter, "Lord of the Dance," © 1963 by Stainer and Bell. Permission granted by Hope Publishing Co., Carol Stream, IL, 60188. All rights reserved.

Chapter Six

MAINTAINING DOCTRINAL BALANCE

*W*hat time is it? The opening line of Charles Dickens's *A Tale of Two Cities* states, "It was the best of times, it was the worst of times." In the Bible the Chronicler reports, "Men of Issachar, who understood the times and knew what Israel should do" (1 Chron 12:32 NIV). The Germans often refer to a particular trend or psychological mind-set as *Zeitgeist*, "the spirit of the times." In *The American Crisis*, Thomas Paine's diagnosis of his generation was, "These are the times that try men's souls. . . . What we obtain too cheap, we esteem too lightly."[1] The Latin phrase *carpe diem* is a challenge to our twenty-first-century doctrinal *Sitz im Leben* or situation in life. The apostle Paul attempted to prepare the church of the *already* for the times of the *not yet* by indicating that "the time will come when men will not put up with sound doctrine. Instead, to suit their own desires, they will gather around them a great number of teachers to say what their itching ears want to hear. They will turn their ears away from the truth and turn aside to myths" (2 Tim 4:3–4 NIV).

These are times when preaching has exchanged its birthright of sound doctrine for an unsatisfying bowl of doctrinal heresy. These are times when preaching has left Joseph's doctrinal bones in Egypt and made its trek to the promised land without them. These are times when preaching can no longer responsibly respond to Joshua's question, "What do these stones mean?" (Josh 4:6 NIV) because too many of its hearers know *what* they believe without knowing *why*.

---

1 *Thomas Paine Reader*, ed. Michael Foot and Isaac Kramnick (London: Penguin Group, 1987), 116.

If preaching fails to reclaim the mantle of sound doctrine and instead neglects the task of balanced doctrinal preaching, geology will be justified in protesting against preaching as the rocks cry out. God is sovereign and uses creation to amplify truth about himself: "The morning stars [sing] together and the sons of God have shouted for joy" (Job 38:7); "the heavens declare the glory of God; and the firmament sheweth his handiwork" (Ps 19:1); "the mountains and the hills shall break forth before you into singing" (Isa 55:12); "and the redeemed of the LORD [must] say so" (Ps 107:2). Preachers of Christian doctrine are resident theologians and are responsible to "earnestly contend for the faith which was once delivered unto the saints" (Jude 3).

Preaching is operating in a time when it has forgotten its alpha, or beginning point. One of the musical principles of Paul Hindemith was that the musicians must always return to the tonic. By this he meant that if a musician was adding, embellishing, shifting, or riffing, the musician must remember always to return to the basic or fundamental music. George Arthur Buttrick, Lyman Beecher Lecturer on Preaching, years ago related an experience that he shared with a preaching audience. One of his preaching students had concluded his sermon and awaited evaluative comments from Professor Buttrick. Buttrick's initial comments were piercingly truthful: if the text had had smallpox, the sermon would not have caught it. To transfer Hindemith's advice to musicians and move it into the arena of preaching: wherever preachers are in the application of the sermon, they must always return to the pulsating heartbeat of the text's original intention.

The former heavyweight champion of the world, Floyd Patterson, was interviewed by an ESPN correspondent. The correspondent knew that Patterson and the reigning heavyweight champion, Mike Tyson, had similar backgrounds in their rise to the top of the boxing world. The correspondent asked Patterson: "If you had the opportunity to say one thing to Mike Tyson, what would it be?" After briefly hesitating, Patterson said, "I would tell Mike to go back to his beginning and review the time when he ate food out of the garbage can and stole for food. This will help keep him from getting the big head."[2] Preachers must return to the tonic of the text if they are to experience balance in their doctrinal preaching.

In his book *Working the Angles: The Shape of Pastoral Integrity*, Eugene Peterson noted that pastors are abandoning their calling. According to his observations, pastors still have their names on the church stationery, keep weekly office hours, and preach the Sunday morning sermon. But they have transformed themselves from shepherds to shopkeepers. According to Peterson, the shops that the shepherds keep are their churches. Questions that concern them are: How can I keep the customers (members) happy? How can I package the goods (sermon) so that the customers (members) will lay out more money? How can I lure the customers (members) from my competitors' shops (churches down the street) to my shop (church)?[3] Paul reminds preachers that they are not to be peddlers of the gospel (2 Cor 2:17). In the words of Jesus, they are to be shepherds who feed the Lord's sheep (John 21:15–17).

Biblical personalities who were greatly used by God had balanced ministries. David could sit down and write hymns, poems, and songs; draw the blueprint for the temple that he would give to Solomon; go out and kill a lion or a bear; and then slay Goliath, the giant. David would encourage both entering into the Lord's gates with thanksgiving for what the Lord had done and then proceeding into the Lord's courts with praise for who the Lord is. Habakkuk chose to sit in silence in the watchtower to wait to see what God was going to say and then sing praises to God with the knowledge that there may not be any cattle in the stall, crops in the field, grapes on the vine, or figs on the tree. Elijah gave a three-and-one-half-year meteorological report to Ahab

---

2 ESPN, May 2005, interview with Floyd Patterson, Cincinnati, OH.
3 Eugene H. Peterson, *Working the Angles: The Shape of Pastoral Integrity* (Grand Rapids: Eerdmans, 1987), 1.

and Jezebel, king and queen of Israel, stating that it would not rain during those years, and then disappeared from their presence. When Elijah reappeared, he called off the drought and challenged the prophets of Ahab and Jezebel to a showdown on Mount Carmel. Jesus could sleep during a storm and wake up and go into the temple and create a storm by driving out the extortionists who were making His Father's house into a den of thieves when it was designed to be a house of prayer for all people.

The Copernican Revolution was an indictment on both the secularist mind-set of science and on the ecclesiastical mind-set of the church. For centuries, science and the prevailing church had believed and proclaimed that the earth was the center of the universe and that God had placed the sun to revolve around the earth. In his famous sermon "The Sun Do Move," John Jasper, the captivating, self-taught preacher of Richmond, Virginia, was affected by this mind-set. The Copernican Revolution had enough conviction and boldness to challenge the scientific mind-set and the ecclesiastical mind-set and say that both were wrong, for God had not placed the sun and the planets around the earth; rather, God had put the sun in the center of the universe.

Doctrinal preaching is out of balance and needs to be called back to a state of balance. What is meant by doctrinal balance? Doctrinal balance is not to be measured by a centrist position, a medium or middle-of-the road position, or a halting or limping between two opinions. Doctrinal balance is better described than defined. Eugene Peterson uses the triangle metaphor to describe a pastoral ministry of balance. Peterson points out that the three lines of a triangle are apparent, but the three angles are essential. The three angles bring the three lines together to form a triangle. Without the three angles there is no triangle. For Peterson the pastoral ministry is triangular in its configuration. The three most discussed lines of the pastoral ministry are preaching, teaching, and administration. These ministries get the most attention. The three angles that are less visible and less discussed are prayer, reading Scripture, and spiritual direction. These three angles of private ministry buttress, support, and enable the three lines of public ministry to become more effective.

Transcendence and Immanence Meet

The first line of balanced doctrinal preaching is formed at the angle where transcendence and immanence meet. Transcendence refers to the truth that God is above us, and immanence asserts that God is with us. Both Henry Mitchell in *Black Church Beginnings* and James Evans in *We Have Been Believers* establish the fact that Africans did not come to America as unbelievers or atheists.[4] Africans believed in the Most High God. In believing that God was above them, they recognized that there was distance between deity and dust, divinity and humanity. The titanic theological struggle was bridging the gap between the *aboveness* of God and the *withness* of God within the unity of one God. How could the same God be both above humanity and dwell with humanity simultaneously? This was the African theological dilemma. Upon being uprooted from their homeland of Africa and transplanted to the soil of America, Africans would adjust and modify the teachings of white Christianity, and white Christianity would assist them in clarifying what they already believed; they had not yet acquired the theological language to articulate what they believed. They would later come to express that the Most High God had a Son and that God in His Son, Jesus Christ, could come out of God and become human without forfeiting His deity. In this mysterious, inscrutable, and inexplicable process, God would become human without losing God's divinity. Theologically speaking, this dynamic is known as the incarnation. "The Word became flesh and took up residence among us. We observed His glory, the glory as the One and Only Son from the Father, full of grace and truth"

4 Henry Mitchell, *Black Church Beginnings* (Grand Rapids: Eerdmans, 2004; James Evans, *We Have Been Believers* (Norristown, PA: Fortress, 1992).

(John 1:14 HCSB). The Son God who came from Father God in the incarnation is the Son God who was forsaken by Father God during the crucifixion. The cry of dereliction reverberated throughout the three realms of earth, heaven, and hell: "My God, my God, why hast thou forsaken me?" (Mark 15:34). In his book *Der Römerbrief*, translated as *The Epistle to the Romans*, Karl Barth dropped a bombshell on the theological world in 1919.[5] For a century liberalism had been amplifying the immanence of God and had lowered the volume of the transcendence of God until it was practically muted. Liberalism anesthetized Christians and made them practically immune to the transcendence of God. The awesomeness of God had vanished from the screen of their minds. Barth led the theological resurgence to reclaim the doctrine of the transcendence of God. Several decades later Barth recognized that although he had sufficiently emphasized the doctrine of the transcendence of God, he had underemphasized the doctrine of the immanence of God. He became intentional about balancing the two in his preaching and writing.

Open theism and process theology indirectly attempt to sever the transcendence and immanence of God. "What God has joined together, let man not separate" (Matt 19:6 NIV). Through their theological mind-sets they attempt to reverse the process of creation and make God in the image of humans when God has made humans in His own image. Theoretically speaking, these two theologies handicap the *Wholly Other*. This is particularly true in the doctrinal category of the omnipotence, or the all-powerfulness, of God. Omnipotence contends that there is nothing that God cannot do. "With God all things are possible," declares Jesus (Mark 10:27). In *Why Bad Things Happen to Good People*, Rabbi Harold Kushner writes in response to the death of his child.[6] He concludes that God sat with his family as a mourner at the funeral

5 Karl Barth, *The Epistle to the Romans*, trans. E. C. Hoskyns (New York: Oxford University Press, 1933).
6 Harold S. Kushner, *When Bad Things Happen to Good People* (New York: Shocken, 1981).

service and wept with the family, for God had done everything He could do prior to the death of the child. Such a doctrinal position flies in the face of the omnipotence of God. Jesus stood at the deathbed of the twelve-year-old daughter of the synagogue ruler, Jairus, who had just died. He told her to rise. She rose, and death died. Jesus met a funeral processional on its way to deposit the body of a young man in the Nain cemetery. He was the only son of his mother, and she was a widow. Jesus touched the top of the coffin and told the son to rise. He rose, and death died. Jesus showed up at the Bethany cemetery four days after the funeral for Lazarus had taken place. He called Lazarus by his name. Lazarus rose, and death died. In the eschaton Jesus will call the saints from their graves, and they will rise. Death will die a final death and will be no more!

These theologies also impair the doctrine of the omnipresence, or the "everywhereness" of God, and the doctrine of the omniscience, or the all-knowingness of God. The doctrines of omnipresence and omniscience argue that God is in all places at the same time and knows everything there is to know about everything. There is no place where God is not. God is so immense spatially that whenever He moves anywhere in the universe, God has to bump into Himself! There is no knowledge about anything that God does not have. Isaiah asserts that God knows the end before the beginning began (Isa 46:10). But process theology and open theism challenge the divine "everywhereness" or omnipresence of God and the "all-knowingness" or omniscience of God by contending that He cannot be in the future or know the future because the future is still unborn and resides within the womb of the "not yet." Yet God is the only one who both dwells in the future and knows the future. God demystifies the mystery of the future, unscrews the inscrutability of the future, and figures out the "unfigurability" of the future. Moses asked Yahweh, "If I am going back to Egypt, the place of my birth and the country where there has been a warrant for my arrest for years, who shall I say sent me?" Yahweh replied, "This is what you are to say to the people of Israel, 'I Aм has sent me to you'" (Exod 3:13–14, author's paraphrase). When someone says "I am," the listener expects the speaker to provide additional information. A sentence seems incomplete when it ends with the words "I am." But when God says "I Am," the sentence is complete because God is complete within Himself, for God is the self-existent God. God is the God who lives up to His claim to be "I Am *who* I Am." God is one noun and three adverbial phrases simultaneously existing in the three tenses of past, present, and future. Although it is grammatically incorrect to articulate God's "I Am-ness," it is doctrinally sound. God is "I Am was." God is before time and even before preexistent eternity. God is "I Am is." God is not in time; time is in God. God is the "Eternal Now." God is "I Am will be." God is on the other side of the future. God sees from the perspective of God's own eternality—*sub specie aeternitatis*.

Process theology and open theism are insufficient for suffering and disinherited people. They need a God who is not in the process of becoming or developing. They need a God who "is" and a God who controls all processes. Often people who are oppressed do not have the technical theological language to relate to the divine attributes of God. Hearkening back to the language of the Negro spiritual, African Americans regularly referred to the omnipotence of God as one who had the whole world in His hands. They understood the omnipresence of God as one who "was so high that you can't get over Him; so low that you can't go under Him; so wide that you can't get around Him; you must come in at the door." They comprehended the omniscience of God as one who could be acknowledged in the lyrics of a Negro spiritual:

> Nobody knows the trouble I see;
> Nobody knows but Jesus.
> Nobody knows the trouble I see;
> Glory hallelujah.

Isaiah announces the omnipotence of God:

> Hast thou not known? Hast thou not heard, that the everlasting God, the LORD, the Creator of the ends of the earth, fainteth not, neither is weary? There is no searching of his understanding. He giveth power to the faint; and to them that have no might he increaseth strength. Even the youths shall faint and be weary, and the young men shall utterly fall: but they that wait upon the LORD shall renew their strength; they shall mount up with wings as eagles; they shall run, and not be weary; and they shall walk, and not faint (Isa 40:28–31).

The psalmist embraces the omnipresence of God:

> Whither shall I go from thy spirit? Or whither shall I flee from thy presence? If I ascend up into heaven, thou art there: if I make my bed in hell, behold, thou art there. If I take the wings of the morning, and dwell in the uttermost parts of the sea; even there shall thy hand lead me, and thy right hand shall hold me (Ps 139:7–10).

Isaiah, the psalmist, and Jesus extol the omniscience of God: "Before they call, I will answer; and while they are yet speaking, I will hear" (Isa 65:24); "All the days ordained for me were written in your book before one of them came to be" (Ps 139:16 NIV); and "Your Father knows what you need before you ask him" (Matt 6:8 NIV).

How do process and open theism theologies respond to the truism of James Russell Lowell?

> Truth forever on the scaffold, Wrong forever on the throne,—
> Yet that scaffold sways the future, and, behind the dim unknown,

Standeth God within the shadow, keeping watch
above his own.[7]

How do process and open theism theologies respond to the
eschatological hope expressed in a song written by the Methodist
pastor and hymnist Charles A. Tindley?

> Harder yet may be the fight,
> Right may often yield to might,
> Wickedness awhile may reign,
> Satan's cause may seem to gain.
> There is a God that rules above,
> With hand of power and heart of love,
> If I am right, He'll fight my battle,
> I shall have peace someday.[8]

Spirit and Word Meet

The second line of balanced doctrinal preaching is formed at
the angle where Spirit and Word meet. The Spirit of God and the
Word of God were married in preexistent eternity. The opening
verses of Genesis 1 established this fact: "In the beginning God
created the heavens and the earth. Now the earth was formless
and empty, darkness was over the surface of the deep, and the
Spirit of God was hovering over the waters. And God said, 'Let
there be light' and there was light" (Gen 1:1–3 NIV).

The prophet Ezekiel stood in the desolate valley of dry bones
with no visible reason to believe that any transformation would
occur through his preaching; but after preaching to these dry
bones, he witnessed the bones making noise, forming skeletal
frameworks, being covered with tendons, flesh, and skin. Finally,
God commanded Ezekiel to preach the word to the four winds

---

7 From James Russell Lowell, "The Present Crisis," in Thomas R. Lounsbury,
ed., *Yale Book of American Verse*, 1912. http://www.bartelby.net/102/128.html.
Accessed October 9, 2006.
8 Charles A. Tindley, "I'll Overcome Someday," 1901.

and tell them to breathe upon the corpses. Ezekiel obeyed God. The Word of God was accompanied by the *ruach*, or the Holy Spirit of God, resulting in the raising of these corpses back to life (Ezek 37:10).

Simon Peter, who had denied his Lord three times following the arrest of Jesus, stands up on the Day of Pentecost, fifty days past that hauntingly unforgettable evening, and boldly preaches the Word. The spoken word by Peter had been preceded by the divine presence of the Spirit in the form of cloven tongues of fire and the rushing mighty wind. After the sermon had been delivered, about three thousand persons were saved and added to the church.

Doctrinal preaching is facing a false dichotomy: Spirit of God or Word of God? This dichotomy has produced a serious dilemma. Churches are lining up on one side or the other. Some take pride in being "Word churches" and others take pleasure in being "Spirit churches." A. W. Tozer, a pioneer in the Christian and Missionary Alliance movement, commonly acknowledged throughout the breadth of his writings that if God took the Holy Spirit out of the world, many churches would continue to do the same things they had been doing twenty-five years after the Spirit's exit and never know the difference. According to Stephen and David Olford, "If the sin of Old Testament times was the rejection of God the Father, and the sin of New Testament times was the rejection of God the Son; then the sin of our times is the rejection of God the Spirit."[9] God as Father is God without human skin. God as Son is God who comes with skin. God as Spirit is God who gets inside of our skin. James Forbes, in his book *The Holy Spirit and Preaching*, charges the contemporary church for being "Holy Spirit shy," or embarrassed by the movement of the Holy Spirit.[10] Some Christians resist and resent being called charismatic. The Greek from which the English term *charismatic* is derived is *charisma*,

9 Stephen F. Olford with David L. Olford, *Anointed Expository Preaching* (Nashville: Broadman & Holman, 1998), 29–30. The Olfords attribute this thought to John Owen.

10 James Forbes, *The Holy Spirit and Preaching* (Nashville: Abingdon, 1989), 21.

which means "favor bestowed, gift."[11] In essence, every believer in the church is a charismatic, in that God has bestowed upon every believer in the body of Christ a gift that is to be used to edify the church (1 Cor. 14:26). Every member has received a spiritual gift by God's grace for the purpose of glorifying God and edifying the church.

Pastors who are comfortable with the members of their churches checking their minds in the vestibule and entering into the sanctuary mindlessly prepare the worship atmosphere for spiritual excesses and biblically unwarranted emotional experiences. Preaching becomes incessant testimonies given from the pulpit that are totally divorced from the text and becomes promises put on their lips without a "thus saith the Lord" certitude. Before one can confidently say "thus saith the Lord," one has to know "what saith the Lord." Many churches virtually have *Ichabod*, "the glory of the Lord has departed," written across the front entrances of their buildings because there is no Word being delivered inside the buildings. In the song "Brethren We Have Met to Worship," George Atkins lyrically voices the inseparability and the unified indispensability of the presence of the Spirit of God and the Word of God engaging the people of God in their praise to God:

> Brethren, we have met to worship and adore the
> Lord our God;
> Will you pray with all your power, while we try to
> preach the Word?
> All is vain unless the Spirit of the Holy One comes
> down;
> Brethren, pray, and holy manna will be showered all
> around.[12]

---

11 Walter Bauer's *A Greek-English Lexicon of the New Testament and Other Christian Literature*, 3rd edition, ed. Frederick William Danker (Chicago: University of Chicago Press, 2000).
12 George Atkins, "Brethren, We Have Met to Worship," 1819.

Where Christology and
an Intratrinitarian Community Meet

The third line of balanced doctrinal preaching is formed at the angle where Christology and an intratrinitarian community meet. Christ inextricably resides within the divine triune community. In mathematics one plus one plus one equals three. This is correct arithmetic, but it is erroneous theology, for it evokes the thought of three gods, which is a contradiction to the *shema*—"Hear O Israel: The Lord our God is one Lord" (Deut 6:4).

Modalism is a heretical doctrine that was condemned by the church over sixteen centuries ago. Modalism teaches that God put on three masks: one mask in the Old Testament as Father; another mask in the New Testament as Son; finally, God has put on a third mask and is in the present world as the Holy Spirit. If God is viewed modalistically, it implies that there was a time when God was not Father because He did not have a Son until the first century when Jesus, the Son of God, was born in Bethlehem. This implies that God was not Father on the first day of creation. The literary corpus of Jonathan Edwards's work testifies that the triune God never acted apart from God's self as existing in a sweet and holy society and forever knowing Himself as Father, Son, and Holy Spirit. The doctrine of the Trinity is the corrective for the heresy of modalism. Instead of modalism's one plus one plus one equals three, the doctrine of the Trinity posits that God is simultaneously working within God's self as Father, Son, and Holy Spirit in the dynamic of one times one times one equals one.

The picturesque portrayal of the creation in James Weldon Johnson's *God's Trombones: Seven Negro Sermons in Verse* is striking and engaging. After nearly seven decades, it continues to be read with great interest and appreciation for both its poetry and its theology. But there is a glaring defect in its imaginative theological anatomy. Johnson suggests that the stimulus behind God's making a human being was that God was lonely. He writes, "And God stepped out on space, And he looked around and said: I'm

DOCTRINE *That* DANCES

lonely—I'll make me a world."[13] There has never been a time when God was lonely. Although humans are not indispensable for the divine completeness, God still desires dispensable creatures so that God may share Himself with them. Neither creation nor humans added anything to God, for God was complete before God ever gave the divine creative fiats, "Let there be" and "Let us make."

The song that once appeared on the first page of several denominational hymnbooks was "Holy, Holy, Holy! Lord God Almighty." Perhaps the relegating of this song from page 1 to several pages toward the back of several of our denominational hymnbooks may be more than a numerical move; it may portray a theological move to indicate a flawed or lessened understanding of Christology within an intratrinitarian community. With profound theology combined with lyrical musicality, Reginald Heber demonstrates the unity of the triune community:

> Holy, holy, holy! Lord God Almighty!
> All Thy works shall praise Thy name in earth and
> sky and sea;
> Holy, holy, holy; merciful and mighty!
> God in three Persons, blessed Trinity![14]

13 James Weldon Johnson, *God's Trombones; Seven Negro Sermons in Verse* (New York: Viking, 1927), 17.
14 Reginald Heber, "Holy, Holy, Holy" 1826; set to John B. Dykes, "Nicaea," 1826.

Chapter Seven

THE JAZZ OF DOCTRINAL PREACHING

Jazz: From Indescribable to Experiential

An elderly Washington socialite came up to Louis Armstrong and asked, "Mr. Armstrong, what is jazz? Can you describe jazz to me?" And he said, "Lady, if you ain't got it, you ain't gonna understand it." Jazz cannot be described or defined; one either feels it or not. Without denying the intellectual aspect of understanding it, if a person does not feel it, that person will never get the sense of why it is so thrilling, exciting, and captivating. So jazz cannot be described in terms of pure, abstract theory. Jazz must be experienced and reflected upon!

In *Blue like Jazz*, Donald Miller looks at faith the way a great jazz musician looks at a simple melody. He sees it as a thing to be explored, a passageway to a treasure trove of even richer melodies, rhythms, and harmonies. Miller recalled:

> I never liked jazz music because jazz music doesn't resolve. But I was outside the Baghdad Theater in Portland one night when I saw a man playing the saxophone. I stood there for fifteen minutes and he never opened his eyes. After that I liked jazz music. Sometimes you have to watch somebody love something before you can love it yourself. It is as if they are showing you the way.[1]

Miller now perceives that there is a relationship between jazz music and Christian spirituality. He explains:

---

1 Donald Miller, *Blue like Jazz* (Nashville: Thomas Nelson, 2003), 14.

141

I was watching BET one night, and they were inter-
viewing a man about jazz music. He said that jazz
music was invented by the first generation out of
slavery. I thought that was beautiful because, while it
is music, it is very hard to put on paper; it is so much
more a language of the soul. It is as if the soul is
saying something, something about freedom. I think
Christian spirituality is like jazz music. I think loving
Jesus is something you feel. I think it is something
very difficult to put on paper. But it is no less real,
no less meaningful, no less beautiful. . . . Everybody
sings their song the way they feel; everybody closes
their eyes and lifts up their hands.[2]

Spirituals as a Musical Ingredient of Jazz

Spirituals were born out of great sorrow. After the Nat Turner
Rebellion of 1831, slaves were prohibited from gathering without their white overseers. To worship freely then, slaves were
forced to go down to the "hush arbors," hidden gathering places
along the riverbanks. Here the sounds of flowing water drowned
out the sounds of their singing. The church during this period
became known as the "invisible institution." The slaves would sing
and pray and praise God. Sometimes they sang about the auction
block where families would be separated forever; sometimes they
sang about the creeping of old age; sometimes they sang about
dying. Everything became a topic for the spirituals.

There was an eschatological dimension in their singing. They
sang about the other side. Their singing was not an opiate for the
masses, as Karl Marx would suggest; they were not afraid of death.
There were things more fearful than death. One of the spirituals
asserts,

2 Ibid., 239.

Oh, freedom! Oh, Freedom over me! . . .
An' be-fo' I'd be a slave, I'll be buried in my grave,
An' go home to my Lord an' be free.

Hope had been feeding on hope for such an indeterminable period of time that hope had dissipated. Hope unborn had died. It was aborted. There was nothing left—no sign of freedom, no sign of getting through this world. They talked about a better place. They would say,

> Got a Savior in de Kingdom,
>   ain't dat good news?
> I'm a goin' to lay down dis world,
> Goin' to shoulder up mah cross,
> Goin' to take it home to my Jesus,
>   ain't dat good news?

"There's a bright side somewhere." Exilic eschatology enabled the slaves to keep their sanity in the midst of dehumanizing circumstances, believing that God's tomorrow would be better than their today.

African Americans sang because they were confident that God was not finished with them or with their world. They hid their messages in cryptic coding and transmitted them on a dual trajectory so that the insider received the intended message and the outsider did not. They would sing,

> Swing low, sweet chariot, coming for to carry me
>   home:
> I looked over Jordan and what did I see?
> A band of angels coming after me.

The slave master would think about heaven; the slave would think about escape. To the insider, Jordan represented Canada, and the chariot, the conductors of the Underground Railroad. The insiders looked for freedom while the outsiders looked for glory. Slaves were talking about a terrestrial, not a celestial, residence.

143

Sometimes they would say,

> I'm goin' home on the mornin' train,
> the evenin' train may be too late,
> I'm goin' home on the mornin' train.

The Underground Railroad is stopping by this morning. Don't wait until this evening. It may be too late. The insider got the message, but the outsider did not. What an ingenious way of exemplifying wisdom! As Jesus said, those who really want to hear will have their ears open to the message, and those who do not want to hear will close their ears and miss the message.

Spirituals amplified a social protest emphasis. These were called sorrow songs. Slaves would talk about the slave master, and he would not even know it. They would sing, "I'm gonna tell God how you treat me, one of these days." The slave master would hear but not understand. Spirituals protested about inequity and injustice in a land where God had made all people equal, had made every individual in His own image, and had written His signature in the fabric of the souls of all people.

In the preface of Dietrich Bonhoeffer's *Life Together*, the translator wrote about a time when Bonhoeffer came to the United States in 1930 to study and eventually to teach at the Union Theological Seminary in New York. Bonhoeffer visited the Abyssinian Baptist Church, which was established in 1808. The choir would sing the spirituals, and the congregation would hear the dynamic preaching of Adam Clayton Powell Sr. Bonhoeffer was touched by the spirituals. He saw a mirroring effect between the African Americans' struggles and those of the Christians in the illegal Confessing Church's seminary in Germany. When he returned to Germany, he taught the Negro spirituals to his students in his underground seminary.

Negro spirituals are a kind of theomusicality. Howard Thurman exegetes the Negro spirituals "Heaven" and "Balm in Gilead."[3] He explains that slaves struggled with the idea of one God and two heavens. They wondered if there must be two heavens because the slave master and his family did not want to be with them on earth, much less in heaven. Yet both the slave masters and the slaves believed they were going to heaven. Were there two heavens? They concluded that there could not be two heavens, for there is only one God. Thus, they reasoned that if there is one God and one heaven, then the slave masters enjoy heaven on earth and suffer eternity in hell. Conversely, the slaves suffer hell on earth but anticipate the delights of eternity in heaven. They would sing,

> I got shoes. You got shoes.
> All God's children got shoes.
> And when we get to heaven, we're gonna put on our
>   shoes.
> We're gonna shout all over God's heaven.[4]

When they got close to the front door of the "big house," they would sing, "Everybody's talking 'bout heaven ain't goin' there/heaven, heaven we're goin' to walk all over God's heaven." It was a way of articulating the eschatological destinies of the oppressed righteous and their wicked oppressors.

Jeremiah asks, "Is there no balm in Gilead, is there no physician there?" (Jer 8:22). This is not a question that is asked to God, nor is it a question that is asked to Israel. It is a question that is asked to the entire ministry of Jeremiah. Jeremiah, you have been preaching and prophesying: Is there no balm in Gilead? Is there no physician there? The Negro slave did an ingenious thing. Thurman said the Negro spiritual took the question mark of Jeremiah and straightened it out into an exclamation point, saying:

3 Walter Earl Fluker and Catherine Tumber, eds., *A Strange Freedom: The Best of Howard Thurmond on Religion and Public Life* (Boston: Beacon, 1998), 150–51.
4 Howard Thurman, *Deep River and The Negro Spiritual Speaks of Life and Death* (Richmond, IN: Friends United Press, 1975).

There is a balm in Gilead, to make the wounded
whole,
There is a balm in Gilead, to heal the sin-sick soul,
Sometimes I feel discouraged, and think my work's
in vain,
But then the Holy Spirit revives my soul again.
There is a balm in Gilead, to make the wounded
whole,
There is a balm in Gilead, to heal the sin-sick soul.

If there was going to be a meeting down in the hush arbor, a
boy would go through the cotton fields delivering water to slaves.
The boy would deliver the message in song:

Steal away, steal away,
Steal away to Jesus!
Steal away, steal away home,
I ain't got long to stay here!

In the evening, slaves would gather in the hush arbor. They would
pray and sing. When they returned to their slave quarters, the
house slaves would sing as they walked by the big house,

I couldn't hear nobody pray
Oh, way down yonder by myself,
And I couldn't hear nobody pray.

This was a way of informing the participants in the hush arbor
meeting that the white master was oblivious of their secret
meeting.

Duke Ellington: A Leading Personality
of the Art Form of Jazz

In *Duke Ellington: A Spiritual Biography*, Jana Tull Steed says:

Ellington's life paralleled the development of jazz. . . .
The amalgam became a new and uniquely American

music—a fusion of European and African elements. Although Duke was without question a jazz musician, he often expressed distaste for the word "jazz," unless it was simply defined as "freedom of expression."[5]

There were times when Ellington's fans were disappointed when he did not replicate the sound of previous musical compositions. This frustrated the Duke. Steed noted, "Failing to appreciate Ellington's continual experimentation, even ardent fans became an irritation when they complained that a piece didn't sound exactly as it did on last year's recording."[6] Duke Ellington always resisted finishing a composition.

The Jazz of Preaching

Gifted minister of music and Christian vocalist, Dr. Sterling Culp, describes jazz as being mainly influenced by the African experience. He looks at five elements of African music and compares them to preaching. According to Culp, the five elements are: (1) call and response, (2) improvisation, (3) syncopation, (4) polyrhythms, and (5) ostinato.[7]

Call and response is one of the earliest forms of African theater. It is like someone playing or singing and a group responding. It is like the antiphonal singing of the seraphim in Isaiah 6. In preaching it is a common expectation for African American preachers to anticipate response to their preaching. It is unrehearsed.

A sermon preached in a black church might begin in a conversational tone. Because of the call-and-response dynamic, it would be lifted from a verbal tone to a cantillation. Soon the preacher and congregation would be preaching together. The King James

5 Janna Tull Steed, *Duke Ellington: A Spiritual Biography* (New York: The Crossroad, 1999), 5–6.
6 Ibid., 60.
7 Conversation with Dr. Sterling Culp, musician, Allen Temple A.M.E. Church, Cincinnati, OH, November 10, 2004.

147

Version had been practically memorized by black preachers, and the literacy rate of slaves increased simply because of the teaching of the Bible to the slave community. Call and response was indeed of the essence of West African music. It provided a basic structure in which to improvise. When slaves came to North America, they encountered European music. They did something to move the singing along; they developed a technique called "lining out." The lead singer would sing the first line of the song, and the congregation would sing the same thing. They would stretch out the lines or lyrics using blues notes. They had all the ingredients necessary for what they called "Singing Dr. Watts." The British hymnist, Dr. Isaac Watts, was the favorite composer of the hymns and songs that blacks sung. Dr. Watts had metricized his songs and made them a lot more singable. By lining them out, they had space and long passages where they could improvise, stretch the notes out, and add vocal embellishments. So there was an encounter between European hymnody sung in a lined-out West African technique combined with sensibility. This was the birth of the musical form called the spirituals.

Improvisation, musically speaking, is "the creation of a musical work, or the final form of a musical work, as it is being performed. It may involve the work's immediate composition by its performers, or the elaboration or adjustment of an existing framework, or anything in between."[8] Spaghetti may be fixed and served many ways. It can be gourmet, like Maggiano's or the Olive Garden; it can be regular Franco American, right out of the can; or it can be homemade, right out of mother's kitchen. Regardless, all spaghetti has a basic form with irreducible components. All spaghetti looks like spaghetti, whether it has mushrooms and extra cheese on it or not. When the preacher preaches, the basic component is the Word of God. There may be variations in the delivery: lecture, whoop, or tune. The proclamation is still the Word of God. The

8 "Improvisation," *Grove Music Online*, http://www.grovemusic.com, accessed June 4, 2007.

improvisation does not affect the declaration or proclamation of the Word of God. When there is no substance, the improvisation is meaningless and purposeless.

Syncopation is defined as "the regular shifting of each beat . . . in which the strong beats receive no articulation . . . or each note is articulated on a weak beat."[9] Loosely defined, it is the irregular accenting of beats. If there are four beats in a measure, without rehearsing, Europeans will generally clap on the first and third beat. Africans will accent on the offbeat, the second or fourth beat. Most Africans find those beats without rehearsal. So, in preaching to white culture, blacks must simply make an adjustment to their beat and feel their liturgical heartbeat. In preaching to black culture, whites must adjust to the rhythm and flow of the congregational atmosphere and allow the congregational current to carry them instead of trying to "swim upstream against the current."

Polyrhythms are "the superposition of different rhythms or meters."[10] In this element people sing in one set of rhythms and clap in another set of rhythms. Spontaneity is what brings polyrhythms into existence without practice. When the congregation gets with the black preacher in rhythm and the organist accents this rhythmic flourish, polyrhythms are at the height of expression. This dynamic involves the minister, members, and musicians with groans, moans, and vocal shouts. The polyrhythms assist in bringing the message to a climax and in helping the message to end on the mountain and not in the valley.

Ostinato is "an accompanimental pattern, usually of one, two, or four bars, repeated continuously beneath precomposed or improvised lines."[11] It is intentional redundancy. Effective preaching is going to repeat certain points and emphases in a message

9 "Syncopation," *Grove Music Online*, http://www.grovemusic.com, accessed May 17, 2007.

10 "Polyrhythm," *Grove Music Online*, http://www.grovemusic.com, accessed May 17, 2007.

11 "Ostinato," *Grove Music Online*, http://www.grovemusic.com, accessed May 17, 2007.

over and over again. Years ago Dick and Jane books were used to teach children: "Look up, baby Sally. Look up, up, up, up, up." The main word of the story was repeated. Whenever a new word was brought in, it was made bold and repeated over and over again.

Jazz: Symphonic Sermonic Implications for Preaching

Kirk Byron Jones, in his book *The Jazz of Preaching*, contends, "Preaching may be enhanced by exploring key elements of jazz and learning to apply those elements to the act of preaching."[12] Christian George of Beeson Divinity School, a jazz artist and a budding theologian and homiletician, sees the following connections between jazz and preaching: (1) earthiness, (2) perpetuity with improvisation in jazz, (3) camaraderie with the Spirit, (4) a collaborative community, (5) organization and organism, (6) spontaneity versus stasis, and (7) Christological components.[13]

The Earthiness of Jazz

B. B. King said in a television commercial in reference to his diabetes, "You know she [diabetes] hurts me so bad." B. B. King felt that one had to understand pain to play the blues. Preachers must preach *through* and *to* trouble, brokenness, incongruities, and woundedness. H. Beecher Hicks Jr. describes it in the title of his book *Preaching through a Storm*.[14] Beethoven was deaf at the end of his life and had to cut off the legs of the piano and put his ear to the ground to hear the vibrations. Jazz has an element of real suffering.

Jazz artists play pieces that are meaningful to people in the audience, some of whom are thinking, *You are playing my life story.*

12 Kirk Byron Jones, *The Jazz of Preaching* (Nashville: Abingdon, 2004), 15.
13 Conversation with Christian George, Birmingham, AL, April 11, 2004.
14 H. Beecher Hicks Jr., *Preaching through a Storm* (Grand Rapids: Ministry Resources Library, 1987).

I live at this particular emotional avenue and relational boulevard.
Charles Haddon Spurgeon once preached a great sermon at his
tabernacle, and a five-year-old little boy came up to him and said:
"Why are you preaching directly to me?" The sermon was theologically intricate, and the boy thought that Spurgeon was preaching
to him. Harry Emerson Fosdick had the same experience. A member met him at the back of the door and asked, with tears running down her eyes, "How did you know?" This happens because
people have different experiences.

Perpetuity with Improvisation in Jazz

Classical music keeps going and comes to a point of conclusion, but jazz is perpetual. If the classical musician continues
beyond the conclusion, it is generally considered negative; but in
jazz a melody line is developing, and it progresses in such a way
that each person, with personal experience and temperament and
style, can vary on that theme perpetually, infinitely, without limit,
until there is a final crescendo, a final climactic moment without an encore. The melody is played through for the first time
by the entire band without embellishment. Then each musician
has a stab at it in his or her own individualistic expression. The
climactic moment comes when they all come together and play
it through the way they did in the beginning. The introduction
matches the conclusion, but there is more "oomph" in the conclusion. There is something different about the final conclusion in
relation to the introduction.

When you improvise, you are not locked into the notes exactly
as they are written on the page. The word *improvisation* comes
from two Latin words: *in* and *provisus*, which means "unforeseen."
Kirk Byron Jones articulately describes improvisation in this manner: "To play improvisational is to play with trusting openness,

151

to go wherever the music wants to go in the moment."[15] Improvisation is spontaneity infused by preparation. In *Notes from a Wayfarer*, Helmut Thielicke tells of going to class with the wrong manuscript. He chose not to go back to get it, so he improvised his lecture effectively. But it was "prepared improvisation."

The tumultuous unrest did indeed subside to some degree, and I pushed my way, unnoticed at first, through the cluster of people to the lectern and immediately began my lecture, saying, "In the last lecture before Christmas I spoke about. . . ." Fortunately, there was no unwelcome applause this time. When I opened my manuscript after freely and briefly recapitulating the previous lecture, I saw to my horror that in the confusion I had brought my notes for the last lecture and had left the right manuscript in the lecturers' common room. For a few shocked moments I circled in nervous oratorical loops above the airfield and considered frantically whether I should admit my mistake and quickly fetch the correct manuscript. But then I thought of the restless crowd outside. An interruption could lead to renewed complications. That something like this had to happen to me of all people at a time when so much was at stake and so many people were watching me sharply to see if I would make a wrong move! Then I pulled myself together and called out to my frightened soul, "With God's help, fly blind!" I put the wrong manuscript away and started to speak without the aid of notes. In doing so, I experienced the truth of what Christian Morgenstern wrote in his gallows song about "greaseproof paper," namely that fear can increase the mind's agility. The necessity of speaking without

15 Kirk Byron Jones, *The Jazz of Preaching* (Nashville: Abingdon, 2004), 80.

notes spurred me on to exceptionally clear formu-
lations and arguments. Nevertheless, I continued to
tremble at the shock and intense concentration for
several hours afterwards.[16]

In her book *A Spiritual Biography*, Jana Steed reported that
Will Marion Cook, a black classical violinist who became Duke's
informal tutor in music theory and composition, advised him to
"find the logical way to develop a melody or voice a chord, then go
around it and let his 'inner self' break through."[17] Kirk Byron Jones
pointed out that Duke Ellington told his band members to play
the notes as written but "to keep some dirt in there somewhere."[18]
By "dirt" he meant improvisation: spontaneous things they did not
plan to do. The Holy Spirit deals in the "dirt area" and provides the
preacher with "editing ecstasy." The Holy Spirit robs us of routine-
ness and predictability. The Duke leaves room for some dirt while
Lawrence Welk plays every note according to the musical score.
When one leaves room for "dirt," the jazz musician no longer
plays the notes; the "dirty notes" play the musician. The preachers'
responsibility is to take people places they have never been before
by being willing to go there themselves. However, this dirt is given
license by being first committed to playing the musical score for
the basic music. I challenge my students to write every word of
the manuscript and then to let the Holy Spirit turn the ink of the
manuscript into the blood of spiritual passion.

I remember reading an article in an African American magazine
about how the popular singing artist Barry White had rebounded
from a career that was at a standstill. He attributed his comeback to learning how to shift his mind without losing his soul.[19]

16 Helmut Thielicke, *Notes from a Wayfarer*, trans. David R. Law (St. Paul,
MN: Paragon, 1995), 200–21.
17 Steed, *A Spiritual Biography*, 48.
18 Jones, *The Jazz of Preaching*, 84.
19 Kevin Chappell, "Barry White: Comeback of the Decade," *Ebony*, May
1995, http://findarticles.com/p/articles/mi_m1077/is_n7_v50/ai_16878130,
accessed May 17, 2007.

He no longer went into the studio with individual players and their instruments. All he took was a computer that housed the instruments. Barry White learned to improvise. The great Charles Bix, Louis Armstrong, Miles Davis, Dizzie Gillespie, and Lionel Hampton knew that when they played jazz, they didn't know exactly what was going to happen. That is why they couldn't play the same chord exactly the same way during a jazz improvisation performance. They didn't feel the same way twice.

On Saturday evening, June 25, 2005, I was sitting in a hotel restaurant in Alexander, Virginia, eating a meal, when a physically challenged African American man struggled to get to the piano stool and started taking people's requests. One guest requested "New York, New York," and he played it. Another requested a Ray Charles number. Before playing each of these songs, he looked into his large black binder and played it according to the music score. He had already informed the dinner guests that if the song was in the binder then he could play it. I requested the Mills Brothers song, "Yellow Bird." He played it also. Then the thought occurred to me that he promised only to play the songs that were in the book. He played by the eye and not by the ear. There was no improvisation, even in his note playing. Preaching must have both an eye and an ear, and there must be freedom to catch the eye of God and to listen in the ear of God during a moment of pregnant silence.

Camaraderie with the Spirit in Jazz

In jazz there are no wrong notes, only wrong resolutions. A resolution is where you end up. You hear a string of notes and wonder where this is going and you end up all right! In this way jazz is likened to the Spirit (cp. John 3:8). Just as there is an inability to describe the mystery of jazz as to where it is going, so the Spirit who searches the deep things of God is unsearchable.

The Jazz of Doctrinal Preaching

Like the Holy Spirit jazz is innate and more powerful than the player/preacher. There is nothing still about jazz; it is movement. It is discovery because each time you play it you are going to discover something; it is creating and creative. It is vibrant and expectant. You expect something to happen. Jazz is always full of surprises. When you are playing jazz, you feel what your audience is feeling. It is communal; it is like call and response in black preaching. When one plays classical music, it is all written down; and one plays it as it should be played. There is less opportunity for improvisation, a disharmonic resolution, or for emotional expression that is not preset by the composer.

In the preaching moment there must be an openness to the movement of the Holy Spirit, who may choose instantaneously to edit and adapt a well-manicured manuscript, thus making the preaching event a fluid rather than a fixed dynamic. The preacher must depart from the manuscript during the moment of spiritual unexpectancy, as a news reporter departs from the prepared news script when receiving a late-breaking news item. It is poor stewardship for the preacher to write various thoughts on paper without any purpose. The sermon is never finished; it is organically alive and lives during its preparation and execution, as well as after the execution, for the "after preacher," the Holy Spirit, preaches to the hearer and the preacher after the benediction.

A jazz musician struggles to find the "invisible notes." The benefit of jazz is that you don't know where it is going. There's such spontaneity with jazz. On the spur of the moment, when one has not had time to prepare, the jazz musician searches and reaches up for invisible notes that are not there and have not arrived. There is no guarantee that they will. The jazz musician knows it is there, but he or she doesn't know where the note is or how to get it. Benny Goodman used to put his clarinet above his head, which is a very irregular thing, and reach up into the unknown to find something tangible. Too many preachers never struggle for words because they are totally dependent on their manuscripts.

There is no discovering anything; everything has been mastered. There is no "Lord prepare me today for what you have prepared for me today." There needs to be an internal moaning and waiting until the Spirit provides that word. This builds the confidence of preachers because preachers know they did not manufacture anything.

This is Paul's message in Romans 8:26: The Holy Spirit makes intercession for us with groans that words cannot express. Doesn't the same apply to preaching? The Holy Spirit takes our intentions to the Lord and interprets them with groans that are too deep for words. Sometimes more is said by what is unfinished in our sentence after struggling for the right word. Are we too dependent upon our vocabulary and not enough on the divine thesaurus? The Spirit steps in our stuck or blank or mental lapses, which is really *pregnant silence*, and we experience incredible clarity instantaneously. That space is uncomfortable and almost unbearable. The pregnant silence, or sacred silence, seems eternal; but it serves as a womb to birth faith so that out of the labor pains of waiting on the Word, God is glorified, and we are edified as we hear ourselves say things that we had not thought of before. Preachers and singers experience this pregnant silence. I once heard a man talking about worship. I shall never forget his words: "When the anointed singer sings, God actually rides on the note, and the Spirit gets into your heart before the note reaches your ear." Perhaps this is what is going on in the preaching moment when preachers find themselves in "sacred stuck places" only to grasp fresh and vibrant thought beyond the struggle.

Jazz musicians must have fun and enjoy themselves together. James Earl Massey calls it "the burdensome joy of preaching." Gardner C. Taylor calls it "the sweet torture of Sunday morning." Sometimes jazz musicians have to create or feel or discover notes while they are having jamming sessions. These notes are not on the page. They may not feel their way into them again. This is totally unrehearsed, and one can see the joy all over their faces as they are shocked and surprised by what they are hearing. And some of them don't even know one another. Jazz music has a capacity to unite people.

Jazz as a Collaborative Community

Jazz is communal music. The musicians are made to be in relationship with the audience. Camaraderie is the meat of jazz. The jazz musicians have fun. It is like they are on a battlefield together, struggling through the same notes. There is beauty on the battlefield because those who are beside them are part of the same music. A musician learns much more; it is a laboratory and concert experience simultaneously. Jazz musicians learn from one another rather than just playing a piece of sheet music. The jazz band is like the body of Christ: the instruments are incomplete without one another. The drums cannot support the melody of the trumpet if there is no trumpet; and, likewise, the trumpet would have no rhythm and beat to follow if there were no drums. So then, jazz is a collection of individual artists producing a collective sound at a conventional moment with a spontaneous spirit. This is truly the image and definition of the kingdom of God. Jazz can influence preaching for the better by creating a dialogical atmosphere. Just as the instruments answer one another, the dancers and crowd respond to the music. For the preacher this dynamic has the potential for producing musicological ministry.

The audience in the jazz concert encourages jazz musicians, and this brings out more in them. The jazz musician sees the lighted-up faces in the audience, and this changes the way he or she plays. This is "call and response" musicality. ABC analyst Michelle Tafoya interviewed Manu Ginobili after the San Antonio Spurs won the NBA championship in June 2005. Ginoboli had had quite a year: he got married, won a gold medal for Argentina, and now had won an NBA championship. Michelle said, "I have never seen you so animated. Why did you motion to the crowd to get with you?" He responded, "Because we needed the power they gave us." Parishioners and proclaimers belong together. Preachers preach so that the church might preach the pastor's message throughout the week in the barber shop, beauty shop, and beyond.

Jazz Organized and Organic

Jazz writes all over the margin and wherever there is space. One of my former preaching students was afraid of losing control of the story and consequently felt uncomfortable about treating a narrative passage in a narrative fashion. We must not try to control the story. Like jazz, let the story roam. God takes our two fish and five loaves and multiplies them so that the members of the church, like the jazz audience, have something to take home with them.

Classical music is technical and well crafted, well ordered, designed, and balanced; the ending has to fit the beginning. Classical musicians have pursued a theme and have been able to trace a concept. But in jazz a good group of musicians can play the same tune a thousand different ways on a thousand different nights without rehearsal. They just seem to come together, merge, and fit together, reach into one another's minds and hear one another's music. It is all spontaneity and immediacy without much preplanning. When jazz musicians and classical musicians come together, the most difficulty is experienced on the classical side because classical musicians have to make significant adjustments to fit in with the jazz players, who are unpredictable. The jazz players probably have greater virtuosity in terms of freedom and improvisation. They will go off on tangents that never occur to the classical musician who thinks that there is merit in preparation and predictability and chaos in immediacy and improvisation.

Classical music is structured to the point that, unless there is a preordained section for improvisation, any deviation is considered negative. There is structure to jazz also. There are chords to play and follow but jazz is also organic and moves around. The structure is fluid and not fixed. Jazz flows and goes wherever it wants. In classical music the object is to interpret as closely as possible the intentions of the composer. If one is playing a sonata by Beethoven, he or she is going to play it as closely as possible to how Beethoven would have wanted it played. One can learn the basic elements, but the beauty of jazz is that one develops it within oneself. It flows out of what one has become, and it flows out of one's experiences. Jazz is less of a prison and more of a field in which the individual musician is given license to roam and discover. Jazz is like preaching in formation, for it never arrives. There is mystery in jazz and preaching. The musician attempts to play notes he or she has never played before.

Jazz as Spontaneity and Not Stasis

Spontaneity is the process of inspiration and risk taking. Stasis is a state of static balance or equilibrium.[20] Jazz musicians are risk takers. They launch off from a point and don't know where they are going to finish up. Roger Salter, a former amateur jazz musician and presently the pastor of the Saint Matthew's Episcopal Church in Birmingham, Alabama, related to me that he went to a Louis Armstrong celebration featuring musicians such as the English trumpeter Pete Smith, who played Louis-style on the trumpet, and Nat Pierce on the piano, among others. After the concert, Salter went backstage to talk to some of the musicians and to get their autographs. He said:

> They were talking about Errol Garner, the pianist, who couldn't read a note of music and had never had a lesson in his life. But he was famous for composing the tune "Estee." He played pure, instinctively, spontaneously, naturally, without a lesson, without a

20 *Merriam-Webster's Collegiate Dictionary*, 10th ed. (Springfield, MA: Merriam-Webster, 1993), s.v., "stasis."

159

tutor. He sat down at the piano and played superbly every time, and it blew professionally trained musicians' minds who were schooled, and even jazz musicians who were able to improvise. One of his admirers, who was not a practicing or convinced Christian, found that he came to believe in God watching Errol·Garner play the piano, because he would see him start off, develop his theme and go into a sort of swirl and curly-queue with music, and think that he'd never get out of this and finish in a proper way and on the right note, though he would bring it all to the most perfect conclusion and everybody would just nod their heads. That made Garner's admirer believe that behind the musician's skill and playing and creativity, there is a divine power. There's a creator; there's an inspirer. It's a matter of launching out in trust.[21]

Jazz is open to any last-minute inspiration because it thrives in the realm of spontaneity; as long as there is a theme, there can always be variation. John Coltrane said, "Change is inevitable in music—things change."[22]

Jazz is open to late, unexpected, inspirational movements of the spirit, which edit out the familiar and insert the unfamiliar. It is a kind of sanctified serendipity. There is mystery in movement. Often the musician does not know where the music is going. When the preacher gets up to preach, the preacher often becomes the follower of the message and not necessarily the initiator. This is also true with the jazz musician. Wynton Marsalis uses jazz as

---

21 Interview with Dr. Roger Salter at Beeson Divinity School, Birmingham, AL, April 24, 2004.
22 John Coltrane, http://www.allaboutjazz.com/coltrane/quotes.htm, accessed May 17, 2007.

a platform to play his trumpet. During a PBS interview, he said, "I close my eyes, and often don't even know where I am going."[23]

This is the spirit of jazz. The jazz musician is prepared and has learned the scales in their variations, but the moment he or she is on the platform is like the moment the preacher is behind the pulpit: the Spirit takes over. There is the free roaming of the Spirit while the manuscript is right before the preacher. Both the musicians and the minister have to keep the door cracked and expect the roaming of the Spirit. Sanctified spontaneity is not directionless spontaneity. "He knows the way I take" (Job 23:10 NASB). Dr. Timothy George, dean of Beeson Divinity School, and I have been formed and informed by Hebrews 11:8: Abraham went out "without knowing where he was going" (NLT). He did not know where he was going, but he wasn't lost because God promised to show him what He had told him. We preach by faith and are looking for something. Abraham looked for a city, and we are looking for a revelation. Neither is concrete at the moment, but we continue to look, and the Spirit testifies when we have found that city or that God-revealed word. Thomas Merton believed that Abraham moved from a state of certainty to a state of risk and trust. Remaining in the sphere of stasis is much more comfortable and much less risky. Magellan defied cartographers, sailed "off the map," and discovered unseen territories. Copernicus defied the prevailing solar system theory and challenged the church and science, thus initiating the Copernican Revolution. Kentucky chaplain Bob Cunningham related to me in an e-mail an article he wrote for his hospital's newsletter titled "Listening for the Gift of Life," which concerned wisdom imparted by George, a man who had been wounded in World War I. George said to Chaplain Cunningham, "My dad always told me two things: (1) When you pray—pray out loud, so God can hear you; and (2) you will never listen yourself into trouble." As preachers, when we stand on that sacred ground listening for the revealed Word

---

23 Wynton Marsalis, PBS interview, January 31, 2001.

during pregnant silence, we must not try to fill that space with an unnecessary word from the terrestrial terrain; rather, we must wait for a revealed Word from the celestial courts of glory.

In an interview with Roger Salter, pastor of St. Matthew's Episcopal Church, Birmingham, Alabama, Salter said:

> In light of my Western European background, one would be a little afraid of the spontaneity, and the jazz approach to preaching. When I was in England I would hear very noted preachers say that it was wrong to get excited and emotional, that you had to impart the message in this calm, understated, dispassionate way. The message had to carry the weight of conviction, and you weren't accompanying it with just your attitude, your excitement.[24]

It is not only the tongue that is in use but the whole personality. Christ came incarnate and preached with His whole being (cp. Luke 4:16–22). We are to love God with all our heart and with all our soul and with all our mind (Matt 22:37). Many preachers are restrained, almost to the extent of crushing emotion and squashing it. Often the desire for decorum kills the message and the way the message is felt.

Things happen in the pulpit that are unexpected. Fred Craddock said to the Lord on his way to the pulpit, "Lord, here goes nothing. Let's see what you are going to do with nothing today." Some preachers want to hold the reins so that they are in complete control, but this is pride and self-trust. It is true that content is more important than structure. The struggle continues between order and spontaneity. We are not only to walk by faith; we are also to preach by faith. When that happens, God ambushes us and takes us by surprise, often during the moment of execution and not just preparation. Our fear is that spontaneity creates the possibility of causalities.

24 Interview with Roger Salter at Beeson Divinity School, Birmingham, AL, April 24, 2004.

Liturgies and standardized forms of worship may have a way of keeping God at arm's length. Our standardized sermons may also serve the same purpose. May everything that happens at every moment of delivery be the result of divine inspiration. One can tell when extemporaneous departures from the prepared material have a sense of fluency and connectedness with the prepared material. In those moments one's faith is edified and God is glorified because the preacher realizes in that moment that this is an exegetical epiphany and a sanctified serendipity. All the stops have to be pulled out, and caution has to be thrown to the wind as one senses something brewing and has a brief second to analyze it and not be intimidated with the question, is it safe? The preacher must go beyond comfort zones and be stretched. People will not grow at a comfortable, safe level. They must also be stretched. The preacher must be taken out of self. The Spirit leads, for no one can come to the Father unless the Spirit draws him or her. Charles H. Spurgeon was known to insist that the preacher should prepare as if there was no Holy Spirit and then preach as if the preacher had never prepared.

Jazz arouses the emotions far more spontaneously and immediately than classical music, which takes reflection. One tends to weigh classical music, and the effect on one's emotions is secondary, whereas jazz grips people instantly. Jazz jerks people into a response, and they become vibrant and alive; their bodies are swaying; their feet are stomping, and their fingers are popping. Wouldn't it be something for preachers to love the Lord and communicate the message the way jazz musicians do it? They have a hobby and a vocation, and preachers have a calling. Preachers should be able to get up with the same verve, vivacity, and winsomeness. The music and the rhythm have gotten into the jazz musicians' systems, and that's why they are vibrating. When Christ gets into our systems, He can make us sway and vibrate and move and speak in the same way.

Augustine talked about *delectare* as a goal in preaching. This term means "to delight." Preaching must be enjoyed and not simply endured. There must be delight in preaching. Preachers who delight themselves in the Lord should also delight themselves in the Lord's gospel. The Latin word *tenere* means "to hold," implying the attention of the listeners. When Jesus finished reading the Scripture in Nazareth, "the eyes of everyone in the synagogue were fastened on him" (Luke 4:20). He held their attention in His reading. Doctrinal preaching that dances gets and holds the attention of its hearers.

Christological Elements of Jazz

Unlike classical music, where there is a conductor on a distant platform, the leader of the jazz band becomes one of the jazz players. The leader struggles with the same notes that fellow band members play. This is a picture of the incarnation. The jazz bandleader plays in the same band and wears the same clothes as the other jazz musicians. This is radically different from classical music and an orchestra. The classical music conductor stands up with a baton and directs without playing a musical instrument. The conductor is needed to direct the musicians' musical entrances and points of departure. They look to the conductor for guidance, but they could play without the conductor if they were as in tune with one another as jazz players are. The jazz band director starts the band but then stands beside the others. The jazz director is in the trenches with the jazz musicians. The jazz director is not center stage but is a part of the process. This is the incarnation. In John 1:14, Christ identifies with us. He is not One who just directs our steps but One who becomes involved with us as Emmanuel. This is the message of Isaiah 53 and Isaiah 7:14. He is not just the Servant who rules but also the Ruler who serves.

Christ is both the classical and the jazz band conductor, for He is transcendent as the classical band director who is above us, and He is immanent as the jazz bandleader who "tabernacles" with us.

164

Minor and Major Chords in Jazz

During a jazz funeral a jazz band leads a slow, plodding procession. People walk or slow march to a somber rendition of "Just a Closer Walk with Thee." On the way to the graveyard, the prevailing sentiment is the loss of life. The recessional from the cemetery carries with it the thought of the gift of life after the body has been deposited in the tomb. A trumpet blows as if it were signaling the entrance of angels in heaven.

The basic component of all music is the triadic chord. A triadic chord consists of three notes: the first note (root note), the third note (middle note), and the fifth note (top note). When the third note is closer to the fifth note, it produces a major chord. The major chord brings about the emotions of hope, happiness, and harmony. But when the third note is just a half step closer to the first note, a minor chord is produced. The minor chord reflects the emotions of dread, doom, and despair.

When there is a jazz funeral in New Orleans, the processional heads toward the cemetery with a slow, plodding rhythm and a song in the minor chord. Sometimes it is Fredrick Chopin's "Funeral Dirge," and the jazz band plays the minor chord to reflect dread, doom, and despair. On the way to the cemetery, the prevailing sentiment is the loss of life. But when the body has been deposited in the cemetery, the jazz band picks up the rhythm of the march and plays a song in the major chord to reflect hope, happiness, and harmony. Oftentimes the song is "When the Saints Go Marching In." A trumpet blows as if it were signaling the entrance of angels in heaven. A deliberate, defiant drumbeat motions for the mourners to become merrymakers, prancing and strutting down the street as they experience their mourning being turned into dancing.

Some songs use both minor and major chords within a single piece of music. Donnie McClurkin's "Stand" is an example. It starts out in the minor mode, asking what you do when everything goes against you. But then the song shifts to the major and the lyric charges, "You just stand."[25]

The Negro spiritual "I Am a Poor Pilgrim" is another example of the integration of minor and major chords. The Negro spiritual begins in a minor key:

> I am a poor pilgrim of sorrow; down here in this
> wide world alone.
> No hope have I for tomorrow; I'm trying to make
> heaven my home.
> My mother has gone to bright glory; my father's still
> living in sin.
> My brother and sister won't own me, because I'm
> trying to make it in.
> Sometimes I'm tossed and driven. Sometimes I know
> not where to roam.

Then hope is awakened in the next stanza as the lyrics shift to the major chord; and hope, happiness, and harmony are on the horizon with these words:

> But I heard of a city called heaven.
> And I'm trying to make heaven my home.

Some renditions consist totally of major chords: all hope, happiness, and harmony. The selection "We'll Understand It Better By and By" is an example:

> We are often tossed and driven on the restless sea
> of time;
> Somber skies and howling tempest oft succeed a
> bright sunshine.
> In that land of perfect day when the mists have rolled
> away,
> we will understand it better by and by.

25 "Stand," Donnie McClurkin. *Donnie McClurkin*, Word Entertainment, 1996.

By and by, when the morning comes.
When the saints of God are gathered home.
We'll tell the story how we've overcome;
for we'll understand it better by and by.[26]

In heaven all songs will be sung in the major chord, for there will be no more night, death, sickness, or sorrow because God will wipe away all tears from our eyes. Every day will be Sunday, and the Sabbath will have no end.

Preservation Hall to Paradise

Preservation Hall is in New Orleans. It is not a spectacular place in appearance. It's a little room with a bunch of elderly musicians getting together to play the old standards that made jazz so popular back in the 1920s and 30s. There is a crowd of perhaps two hundred people waiting to get in that little room. On a typical day it will take three or four hours standing in line before one finally gets in the room. It will be hot in that room, and the musicians will be playing the classics of Dixieland that made jazz popular as a genre. Their chief goal night after night is to try to preserve this music. This is a traditionalist party and interest. They don't play or permit any new jazz to be played there. These musicians are from the roots of jazz; they were playing back in the 1920s. This gives them credibility because the audience knows they were there.

Jazz anticipates paradise, when the saints of God are present, who will be in the presence of the Lord for eternity. Believers will transition from "*hitherto* hath the LORD helped us" to "*henceforth* there is laid up for me a crown of righteousness" (1 Sam 7:12; 2 Tim 4:8). They will transition from the "*some more*" experience of separation, sickness, and struggles to the reality "*no more*" death, mourning, crying or pain (Rev 21:4; 22:5). Paradise believers will see the desire of the ages, for they will see the face of the Lord.

26 Charles A. Tindley, *This Far by Faith: An African American Resource for Worship* (Minneapolis: Ausburg Fortress, 1999), 206.

EPILOGUE

*J*n the book *When Life and Beliefs Collide*, Carolyn C. James uses the metaphor of a war zone to stress the importance of doctrine and theology as the serious Christian engages in spiritual warfare. The serious Christian makes an effort not only to advance the kingdom of God through witness but also to survive the aggressive attacks of demonic forces intent on assassinating spiritual well-being. She writes:

> When faith is stripped to the bone and all our props and crutches are gone, our knowledge of God—that He is good and is still on the throne—is the only thing that keeps us going. Our courage and determination in battle hang on our understanding of God's character. Soft theology won't sustain us on the battlefield. Marching into battle with superficial, false, and flimsy ideas of God is like going to war with a popgun tucked under your arm. When fatigue hits and still the battle rages, it makes all the difference in the world to know that God's plan is in place, even here. The thought that He has temporarily surrendered His sovereignty to someone else undermines our confidence, drains us of courage, and weakens our hope. None of us can afford a theology that cannot withstand the pressures of the war zone that fits only within a world of comfort and pleasure, where all our ducks are in neat rows and the pieces fit neatly

together. We are called to be soldiers, to enter the war zone, to feel the heat of battle for ourselves and for each other, and to see God more clearly within the context of our struggles.[1]

During the evaluation of student sermons at Beeson Divinity School, I regularly ask, "Where is the eschaton in this text?" I want the student to see that the Bible was written to be understood backward: that God had the end in mind even before the beginning, Revelation 22 even before Genesis 1. This enables believers to see the Scriptures from God's point of view and to understand that God never *reacts* to anything within the creative realm; He always *pre-acts*. That is, God always acts before there is anything to act upon! Isaiah envisioned this reality when he declared that God knew the end before the beginning began (cp. Isa 46:10). This is the reason believers should trust in the foreknowledge of God when they pray, for God answers before we call (cp. Isa 65:24), and God knows what we are going to ask before we ask (cp. Matt 6:8). The arrest of Jesus, the Son of God, was not a surprise to the Father, for Luke reports that He was handed over to the Jewish leaders by God's set purpose and foreknowledge (Acts 2:23–24). Even the death of Jesus was foreknown in the counsel of preexistent eternity. John draws back the curtain of divine mystery and permits us to see a divine disclosure of Jesus, the Lamb of God who was slain from the foundation of the world (Rev 13:8). In the mind of God the Father, Jesus the Son of God was slain on Mount Calvary before Abraham killed the ram, a substitute for his son, on Mount Moriah. Calvary preceded creation, which indicates that in God's mind Calvary was not plan B, an afterthought; Calvary was plan A, a forethought. In eternity past Jesus, the second Adam, died before the first Adam was created. The tree on Golgotha was planted in the soil of preexistent eternity

---

1 Carolyn C. James, *When Life and Beliefs Collide* (Grand Rapids: Zondervan, 2002), 95.

before the tree of the knowledge of good and evil was planted in the garden of Eden.

The exegetical escort and the doxological dancer are living metaphors whose service will extend beyond terrestrial terrain. These metaphors will be employed in the celestial courts of glory. They are living, even *eternal* metaphors. When the saints of God shall stand on the heavenly shore and wring the waters of tribulation from the hem of their garments, these metaphors will be in existence. The Bible, the written Word of God, that has served as our compass to guide us from earth's sorrows to heaven's joy, will be opened and used as a barometer for the righteous at the judgment seat of Christ, and the unrighteous at the great white throne of judgment. The Spirit will say, "Come!" The bride, which is the church of Christ, will also issue heaven's great invitation, "'Come.' Let anyone who hears this say, 'Come.' Let anyone who is thirsty come. Let anyone who desires drink freely from the water of life" (Rev 22:17 NLT). Jesus, the Son of God, will appear in the eschaton riding on a white horse; His eyes will be like blazing fire; many crowns will be on His head; He will be dressed in a robe dipped in blood; and His name will be the Word of God. The incarnate, living, and revealed Word of God will for eternity remain the subject of our exegesis. Believers who in their earthly life had been escorted to the Christ, the incarnate Word of God, will be escorted by Christ, the revealed Word of God, for the purpose of praising and glorifying the Father. The Westminster Shorter Catechism we will have read on earth will be realized in its fullness in eternity. "Amazing Grace" was right:

> When we've been there ten thousand years,
> Bright shining as the sun,
> We've no less days to sing God's praise
> Than when we first begun.

I believe being in the presence of Christ for all eternity will stimulate saints to dance.

Epilogue

John gives us a panoramic preview of the future state of eternity and the praising and glorifying of the Lord that will take place as a result of the victory He has given the saints over demonic forces:

> And I saw what looked like a sea of glass mixed with fire and, standing beside the sea, those who had been victorious over the beast and his image and over the number of his name. They held harps given them by God and sang the song of Moses the servant of God and the song of the Lamb: "Great and marvelous are your deeds, Lord God Almighty. Just and true are your ways, King of the ages. Who will not fear you, O Lord, and bring glory to your name? For you alone are holy. All nations will come and worship before you, for your righteous acts have been revealed" (Rev 15:2–4 NIV).

If Miriam and the women danced on the other side of the Red Sea as they sung the song of Moses in response to the victory God had given Israel over their enemy, Pharaoh and his armies, it is most probable that the saints of God will join in jubilant dancing as they sing not only the song of Moses but also the song of the Lamb who has given them victory over their enemy, the devil, in a land where there will be "no more sea." Doxological dancing will not be reserved solely for the earthly journey; it will be resumed during our heavenly rendezvous.

In his great hymn, "How Great Thou Art," Stuart K. Hine accurately embodies the sentiments of the saints of the ages as they stand in tip-top anticipation awaiting the coming of their Lord: "When Christ shall come with shout of acclamation and take me home, what joy shall fill my heart! Then I shall bow in humble adoration, and there proclaim, 'My God, how great thou art.' Then sings my soul, my Savior, God, to thee: how great thou art, how great thou art! Then sings my soul, my Savior God to thee: how great thou art, how great thou art!"[2] Until then, may we escort hearers into the presence of Christ for the purpose of transformation so that in the eschaton they can join the innumerable hosts marching to Zion singing, "They have washed their robes and made them white in the blood of the Lamb" (Rev 7:14, NIV).

Since preaching is an act of worship, the goal of every preacher should be to preach so that the congregation will preach the Sunday morning message in beauty salons and barber shops, employment circles and recreational facilities, at home and abroad. Peter Taylor Forsyth poetically depicts preaching as "the organized hallelujah of an ordered community."[3] May we escort the hearers into the presence of God with the Word of the Lord as we dance before Him in our preaching!

2 "How Great Thou Art," words by Stuart K. Hine, © Copyright 1953. Renewed 1981 by Manna Music, Inc, 35255 Brooton Road, Pacific City, OR 97135. International copyright secured. All rights reserved. Permission granted.
3 Peter Taylor Forsyth, *Positive Preaching and the Modern Mind* (New York: Armstrong, 1907), 95.

Sermon 1

"THE OTHER SIDE OF GRACE"
TEXT: 2 CORINTHIANS 12:1–10[1]

And even in our sleep pain that cannot forget,
falls drop by drop upon the heart,
and in our despair, against our will,
comes wisdom to us by the awful grace of God.[2]

These are the words of Aeschylus, sixth-century BC playwright and father of Greek tragedy. They are words that stabilized Robert F. Kennedy during the aftermath of the assassination of his brother, President John F. Kennedy. They are also the words that were referred to on April 4, 1968, when Robert F. Kennedy arrived in Indianapolis to deliver a speech as he campaigned for the presidency of the United States. He was informed that Martin Luther King Jr. had been assassinated in Memphis, Tennessee. He was encouraged to disband the people, to call off the campaign, not to deliver the speech, but he chose to go forth with it. And, as he stood there, he did not use his prepared speech but chose to speak from his heart. He informed those gathered,

---

1 Unless otherwise indicated, Scripture in this sermon is quoted from the Holy Bible, New International Version, copyright © 1973, 1978, 1984 by International Bible Society.
2 Aeschylus, *Agamemnon: Three Greek Plays*, trans. Edith Hamilton (New York: W. W. Norton, 1937), 170.

who loved peace and justice, that Martin Luther King Jr. was killed in Memphis, Tennessee. During his extemporaneous speech, in a slight misquote of Edith Hamilton's translation of these lines from Aeschylus, Kennedy said, "In our sleep, pain which cannot be forgotten falls drop by drop upon the heart until, in our own despair, against our will, comes wisdom through the awful grace of God. These words have been used as one of the inscriptions at the Robert F. Kennedy gravesite in Arlington National Cemetery.

I think they are words Paul would affirm, for Paul was in pain when he wrote 2 Corinthians 12:1–10. There was a stake driven, there was a spear driven in the flesh, and it was against Paul's will; for in Paul's despair he cried out three times, "Take it away from me," and the Lord gave him wisdom by saying, "No, Paul, I will give you something better. My grace is sufficient for you, and my strength is made perfect in weakness" (v. 8). In verse 9, Paul is saying that believers cannot have power unless they have experienced the pain predicament involved in following Jesus: no pain, no power. "I take pleasure in my weaknesses that the power of Christ may rest on me" (v. 9). Also like Aeschylus, Paul learned wisdom through the *awful grace* of God, for he declared in verse 10, "When I am weak, then I am strong." When I am weak and recognize that I am totally dependent on God, at that moment I open myself to God's strength.

Aeschylus talks about the awful grace of God. Is this the inception of insanity? Is this a portrait of dementia? Or does he provide some profound

insight? In Luke 16:8, Jesus talks about the unjust
steward. He does not commend the steward for
being dishonest. He does cite his ingenuity in
terms of how he used the given resources. Jesus
was saying that the people of this world are wiser
in dealing with their own kind than are the people
of light. Is it possible that this pagan Aeschylus has
picked up on an aspect of grace that we often avoid
and don't want to mention and calls it "awful" in
order to teach us something?

We talk about grace always benevolently but sel-
dom malevolently. Grace has furnished the theme
for many of our hymns and gospel songs.

> Marvelous grace of our loving
>   Lord,
> Grace that exceeds our sin and our
>   guilt,
> Yonder on Calvary's mount
>   outpoured,
> There where the blood of the Lamb
>   was spilt.
> Grace, grace, God's grace,
> Grace that will pardon and cleanse
>   within;
> Grace, grace, God's grace,
> Grace that is greater than all our
>   sin.

This is benevolent grace.

> Amazing grace shall always be my
>   song of praise
> For it was grace that bought my
>   liberty;

I do not know just why He came to
love me so,
He looked beyond my fault and
saw my need.[3]

This is benevolent grace.

Through many dangers, toils and
snares
I have already come.
'Twas grace that brought me safe
thus far
and grace will lead me home.

This is benevolent grace, and benevolent grace is amazing grace. We talk about grace in Scripture in an affirming way. "And Noah found grace in the eyes of the LORD" (Gen 6:8). "By grace are ye saved through faith" (Eph 2:8). This is benevolent grace. But what about malevolent grace? Have you ever noticed that in Hebrews 5:8, Jesus, though He was a Son, learned obedience through suffering? Isaiah states in Isaiah 54:7–8, " 'For a brief moment I abandoned you, but with deep compassion I will bring you back. In a surge of anger, I hid my face from you for a moment, but with everlasting kindness I will have compassion on you,' says the LORD your Redeemer." Jesus Himself is tempted by the devil after His glorious baptism (Matt 3:17–4:1).

Awful grace, amazing grace. Could they coexist within the God of the universe? Is it possible that the awful grace of God could be the other side of the coin of the grace of God within the currency of the divine economy of God? Is it possible that

3 Denise Rambo, "He Looked beyond My Fault and Saw My Need" (Nashville: John T. Benson, 1968). Permission granted.

we will never really appreciate the amazing grace of God until we have experienced the awful grace of God? Is it possible that the awful grace of God prepares us through negative circumstances for the amazing grace of God that promotes the will, the design, and the imprint of God in our lives? Is it possible that C. S. Lewis is correct when he refers to God's mercy not as "tender mercies" but as "severe mercies"?

Jacob experienced a great blessing. His name is changed. No longer is his name trickster, supplanter, or wrestler. His name is changed to Israel, which means "let God rule." From "wrestler" to "let God rule." That's amazing! But Jacob has to suffer dislocation before he enjoys the transformation of a new name. He had told the angel, "I will not let you go until you bless my soul." Dislocation is a prelude to transformation. There can be no transformation without dislocation. Is it possible that when you look at Joseph you see both amazing and awful grace? I know we love to read Genesis 50:20, "Brothers, you meant it unto me for evil, but God meant it unto me for good." But Joseph wasn't saying this twenty years earlier when he was put in the pit by his brothers. Joseph wasn't saying this when he had a phony molestation charge put on him by Potiphar's wife. He wasn't saying this when the chief cupbearer forgot him for two years (Gen 40:23). But when he looked back, what appeared to be awful turned out to be amazing because he became a potentate in Egypt and a savior for his people. Job describes the inextricability of awful and amazing grace in this manner: "God deposited in my account, and God made a withdrawal from my account. The Lord has given and the Lord has taken away." Conclusion: "Blessed be the name of the LORD" (Job 1:21, author's paraphrase).

On the Damascus road Paul had to lose his sight in order to get his sight. In Acts 12, two apostles of the inner circle, James and Peter, experience two different outcomes. Peter is spared. James is killed. An angel is sent to deliver Peter, but no angel is sent to deliver James. We often make a great mistake in reading Psalm 23. We're often in such a rush to get to the banquet table (v. 5) that we can sit before the table that's been prepared for us, have our heads anointed with oil, and our cups overflowing; therefore, we try to go around the valley of the shadow of darkness (v. 4). We can't get *to* the banquet table (v. 5) until we go *through* the valley of darkness (v. 4). This is a portrait of a journey of both amazing grace and awful grace. Dr. James Earl Massey calls preaching "burdensome joy," and Dr. Gardner C. Taylor refers to preaching as "sweet torture of Sunday morning." The "joy" is amazing, and the "burden" is awful. The "sweetness" is amazing, and the "torture" is awful. There is no antithesis, only a "sanctified synthesis."

In Job 37:22 Elihu refers to God as being "terrible majesty" (KJV). It is like experiencing "trembling" and "adoration" simultaneously as believers bow before the Sovereign Lord. In the Hebrew the word for "majesty" is the word *kavod*. It means "glory" or "honor." We like that: glory and honor. But the word for terrible in Hebrew is the word *norah*. It is translated "awesome." God is the actor doing the acting, for God is putting the awe in the awesome, and God is putting the terror in the terrible; therefore, God is "terrible majesty." In 2 Corinthians 12 there's both: *kavod* and *norah*.

Luther criticized the scholastics for not having a full theology. He said that they did not have a theology of the cross, only a theology of triumph, of evidence, of achievement. According to Luther they did not have any shadows in their theology. They needed a theology of the cross as well as a theology of glory.

Both are evident in 2 Corinthians 12. Paul loved the Corinthian church. He spent eighteen months there building it up. Somewhere between his first and second letters written to Corinth, some false teachers tried to discredit Paul as an apostle. So they began to talk about his credentials: "You're not really a super apostle. You are an apostle born out of season. A Johnny-come-lately apostle. You ought to come to the table and debate with us. We have a lot of things to boast about. What can you boast about?" And Paul said in 1 Corinthians 1:31, "Let him who boasts boast in the Lord." He stated, "Whether you eat or drink or whatever you do, do it all for the glory of God" (1 Cor 10:31). He had worked harder and suffered more than his critics. He had been whipped by the Jews five times, shipwrecked three times, beaten with rods three times, stoned once, been in danger on land and sea and had faced challenges among false brothers. If he really wanted to boast he could; but he chose not to do so. In 2 Corinthians 12:1–6 he talks about an experience autobiographically—"I knew a man in Christ"—as if the man he knew was someone other than himself. He chose not to talk about this person in first-person singular but rather in third-person

179

singular, referring to the man as "he" or "him." He spoke this way to avoid the appearance of boasting. He said: "I knew a man about fourteen years ago who was called up to the third heaven, to paradise, the very throne of God. He saw things that caused God to put a divine verbal restraining order on him. What he saw had to remain inexpressible, and what he heard had to remain unspeakable. Whether he was caught up in the body, I don't know, or whether he was caught up in the spirit, only God knows." Paul says, "I knew this man. If I wanted to boast, I could boast, and I would not be lying: I'd be telling the truth. I would not be a fool because what I'm saying is really true."

Now these false apostles evidently had hurt Paul because, in the middle, between 1 Corinthians and 2 Corinthians, Paul sends Titus with what scholars called a "severe letter." Paul has said, "You've got to reject this false teacher." When Paul visits Corinth, someone in the congregation withstands him to his face, and no one from Corinth defends him. Paul is now sending Titus. Titus comes back and gives the reports. Paul writes 2 Corinthians to these individuals. He said, "Now because of these unsurpassed, unprecedented experiences, God put a gag order on me. God said, 'I've got to give you something to keep you from being exalted above measure. I'm going to put a stake in your flesh.'" Scholars have spent years trying to figure out what the thorn was. Paul didn't say anything about what he saw up there. He didn't say anything about what the stake was. Paul knew that Enoch walked with God, was translated, and never came back to report what he saw in paradise. Elijah was taken to heaven by a fiery chariot, pulled by horses of fire, with reins of fire, and came back for a brief visit with Moses and Jesus on the Mount of Transfiguration (Luke 9:30). They talked about the "*exodon*," or the exodus— the decease that was going to take place in Jerusalem. Unlike Peter and John, Paul cannot speak of what he has seen and heard (Acts 4:20).

Paul said, "There was given me a thorn in my flesh" (v. 7). What is this thorn? Some have said that Paul was a first-century rabbi who was married and that the thorn was his wife. John Chrystosom, the fifth-century patriarch and bishop of Constantinople, said that Alexander the coppersmith was the thorn. From Gregory the Great to Thomas Aquinas, some have said that it was *stimulus carnis*, stimulation of the flesh, penile propensity, sexual temptation. John Calvin and Martin Luther have said that it was spiritual temptation. Others have said it was scoliosis of the spine, while still others have said that it was malarial fever. It could have been eye trouble, for in Galatians 6:11 Paul points out that he was writing this letter in large letters with his own hand. The speculation continues to this day. But Paul doesn't tell us what the thorn is. The question is not, what is the thorn? It's a theological question: why the thorn? Paul says it was given to him to "keep me from being conceited because of these surpassingly great revelations."

I was sitting at the Fairmont Hotel in Dallas, Texas getting ready to preach at the E. K. Bailey International Conference on Expository Preaching, and the Lord asked me this question: "How high can I lift you without losing you?" A. W. Tozer was asked, "Why did God use A. B. Simpson to serve as a major architect in the formation of the Christian and Missionary Alliance movement? There was nothing spectacular about him." A. W. Tozer said, "Because God finally found someone that He could trust with His glory." Some will not fail in ministry because of moral failure. Some will fail because they could not be trusted to glorify God with their God-given giftedness for ministry. God is sovereign. God ordered the thorn, and a demonic angel delivered it.

The most difficult part of the Serenity Prayer is "Lord grant me the serenity to accept the things I cannot change." How do you deal with things you can't change? How do you deal with things you can't get rid of? How do you, like Jacob, handle the limp that won't go away? According to Max Lucado in the book *In the Grip of Grace*,[4] God would rather for us to limp in humility than to strut in pride. What do you do when you are given a limp? I tell you what God did: Paul was given grace to nurse it. Paul had asked the Lord three times to take the thorn away. The Lord said, "No, I'm not going to take it away from you. My grace is sufficient for you. I am enough for you. Paul, what I'm trying to do is to use this to keep you down where I can use you so I can conform you to my image." God often gives us these stakes and spears in our flesh, hindrances so that they might turn into helps, intrusions so that they might become invitations, obstacles so that they can be transformed into opportunities, and problems that can be recycled into possibilities. If we want to go into the throne

---

4 Max Lucado, *In the Grip of Grace: Your Father Always Caught You—He Still Does* (Dallas: Word, 1996).

room, we must first go into the thorn room, for that's where Jesus went. There He is in the garden of Gethsemane. He prayed three times, "Father, if it's possible, let this cup pass from Me." And God's no was louder than His yes. His will became lost in the Father's will. Paul complained of a thorn, but his Lord wore a crown of thorns. It was awful that Friday. So awful that He said, "My soul is exceeding sorrowful, even unto death." It was an awful Good Friday. But if you close the book on Friday, grace is incomplete. It took the awfulness of the crucifixion of Good Friday to bless us with the amazing result of the resurrection on Sunday morning. That Sunday morning this same Jesus, who died on Friday, got up with all power in His hand.

One of these days, when we leave these earthly shores, take off mortality and put on immortality; one of these days when we stand before God and wring out the blue waters of tribulation from the hem of our garments, we shall see traces of the awful grace of God and the amazing grace of God. We shall see both realities when we walk on streets of gold. Gold is not found in the outlying environment. Gold has to be dislodged from a large rock with great pressure and put in a fiery vat. The fire will separate the gold from the "slag" and the extraneous material. When we shall walk on streets of gold, we will be reminded of the tribulation we had to experience before we entered into the kingdom of God. When we walk through pearly gates, it will represent the amazing grace of God and the awful grace of God. Pearls are not found on the streets under the firmament of the sky. A piece of sand or some other irritant gets embedded within the delicate tissue of the oyster. The oyster gets some relief by secreting fluids that will harden, form a pearl, and serve as the buffer from the pain of the irritant. The more secretion, the larger the pearl gets. When we walk through the pearly gates, it will represent that we've come through the awfulness of the grace of God, but the amazing grace of God is ushering us through the gates of pearl. And when we bow down at Jesus' feet, we'll see the awful effects of awful grace. We will recognize Him by the wound in His side. But we will rise and crown Him King of kings and Lord of lords.

> Through many dangers, toils and
>   snares
> I have already come;
> 'Twas grace that brought me safe
>   thus far,
> And grace will lead me home.

"LIVING ON THE EDGE OF WHATEVER HAPPENS"
TEXT: PHILIPPIANS 1:1–2, 12–13, 19, 27[1]

T o live a "whatever-happens" existence is not to resign one's self to cynicism, to disillusionment, to nihilism, or to skepticism; but rather it is to embrace Providence, the superintending hand of God that guides us even through the mist of mystery. This is what gives us peace when we can't figure out the "un-figure-out-able." When we walk through the maze of confusion and can't see clearly as we go, we know that the hand of God still leads us. This reality echoes the sentiment of one of our favorite hymns:

> Great is Thy faithfulness, O God
> my Father . . .
> Morning by morning new mercies
> I see.
> All I have needed Thy hand hath
> provided;
> Great is Thy faithfulness, Lord,
> unto me![2]

It embraces the remarks of James Russell Lowell:

> Truth forever on the scaffold,
> Wrong forever on the throne,—

---

1 Unless otherwise indicated, Scripture in this sermon is quoted from the Holy Bible, New International Version, copyright © 1973, 1978, 1984 by International Bible Society.
2 Thomas O. Chisholm, "Great Is Thy Faithfulness," 1923.

185

Yet that scaffold sways the future,
and, behind the dim unknown,
Standeth God within the shadow,
keeping watch above his own.[3]

All of us start out as zeros, but we are not nihilists. *Nihilo* means "nothing." *Creatio ex nihilo* means that God created the world out of nothing. God brought something out of nothing. God came from nowhere because there was nowhere to come from. God stood on nothing because there was nothing to stand on. God took nothing and flung it out into nowhere and told it to stay there. God took a sun, put it in the sky without any upright, put the planets in a merry-go-round system around the sun, and they haven't collided since the day of creation. God made the floating, fluffy, fleecy white clouds. God carpeted the earth with green grass. God has given us everything that we see, and yet we started off with nothing.

If God can start off with nothing in nature, look at our lives. Some were rejects. Some were voted in high school the most likely not to succeed. Some were given up to die. Some were not supposed to be walking around. Some were not supposed to speak again. Some were not even supposed to know that they were in the world. But God took their nothingness and made something glorious. God has taken some from the basement of debasement and made something beautiful out of their lives. God has taken our miserable existence, our wrecked marriages, and our diseased bodies and moved us

3 From James Russell Lowell, "The Present Crisis," in Thomas R. Lounsbury, ed., *Yale Book of American Verse*, 1912. http://www.bartelby.net/102/128.html. Accessed October 9, 2006.

from transition to transformation. We're not nihilists. We just believe in a God who can take nothing
and make the impossible possible. This is the kind
of existence that the apostle Paul practiced. It is
particularly visible in the first chapter of the letter
written to the Philippians.

Seven hundred and fifty land miles away the
apostle Paul wrote a letter from a prison. He said
in chapter 1, verse 1, "Paul and Timothy, servants
of Christ Jesus." In several of the other letters, it's
Paul the apostle. There's a title that prefaces this
letter. But because this is his favorite church, his
sweetheart church, he drops the title and just says
"servant." As Dr. Sandy Ray eloquently put it many
years ago, "Testimonies are greater than titles."

A profound statement in Luke 3:1–2 is often
overlooked. It somehow blends in with the nomen-
clature scenery of that text. "In the fifteenth year of
the reign of Tiberius Caesar—when Pontius Pilate
was governor of Judea, Herod tetrarch of Galilee,
his brother Philip tetrarch of Iturea and Traconitis,
and Lysanias tetrarch of Abilene—during the high
priesthood of Annas and Caiaphas, the word of
God *came* to John son of Zechariah in the desert"
(emphasis mine).

When God got ready to appoint a precursor—
a forerunner, a public address announcer—for his
Son, God skipped the imperial throne in Rome.
God bypassed the governor in Judea, the governor
in Galilee, the governor in Abilene, the governor
in Iturea and Traconitis, and even the high priest
in Jerusalem and went out in no-man's-land where
there was a babbler. God selected someone who
had never finished divinity school, didn't have a

seminary degree, and had not been licensed by a church. God told John the Baptist, "Go and tell the people that the Son of God is coming. Repent, for the kingdom of heaven is at hand."

God is not interested in our titles. Titles don't preach. I teach in a divinity school, but degrees don't preach. When put on a wall they'll get yellow, but they won't preach. God will take people who are sold out for God, who have no recognition, refinement, or polish, establish them and make them a great voice for God.

"Paul and Timothy, servants of Christ Jesus, to all the saints who are in Christ Jesus at Philippi." In Christ Jesus at Philippi! In Christ Jesus at Philippi! Paul was saying, in essence, that your permanent address is in Christ Jesus. Your varying zip code is at Philippi. Your zip code changes, but your address in Christ is permanent.

Paul found that out in Acts 16:6–7 when he was making his second missionary journey with Timothy and Silas. He found out that the Spirit of God, instead of giving him the Great Commission to go into all the world to preach the gospel to every creature, gave him the great *prohibition*. He wanted to go to Asia Minor and Bithynia, but the Spirit said no. Paul could have been a blessing in both places, but the Spirit said no. The zip code is subject to changing!

Finally Paul wound up in Troas. By this time the ancient city of Troy had probably seen its glory fade away. How do we handle Troas when we've wanted Asia Minor and Bithynia? If we're going to get to Philippi and hear the Macedonian call at night, "Come over and help us," we've got to spend

188

some time at Troas. Some want Philippi but don't want to spend any time in Troas. If we're too big for Troas, can God use us in Philippi?

Brothers and sisters, the greatest challenge we will face is not the challenge of God opening a bad door that we must go through while other good doors are appealing and tempting. The struggle is not between the good door and the bad door but between the good door and the best door. That's our greatest challenge. God will close some doors (Bithynia and Asia Minor) to get us to pay attention to the best door (Philippi).

We keep singing, "Order my *steps* in your Word, dear Lord," but sometimes God orders our *stops,* and we just need to get within a rhythm of sanctified synchronization so that we are in step with God and *step* when God says step and *stop* when God says stop. Our address of being in Christ is permanent, but the zip code of our location of Christian service is subject to change.

"Paul and Timothy, servants of Christ Jesus, To all the saints in Christ Jesus at Philippi . . . : Grace and peace to you from God our Father and the Lord Jesus Christ" (Phil 1:1–2).

This letter is a christologically soaked and saturated letter. It's about Christ, and Paul was living on the edge of Providence, the edge of "whatever happens." Hear what he had to say in verse 12: "Now I want you to know, brothers, that what has happened to me has really served to advance the gospel."

Paul was the optimal optimist. Paul was the quintessential enthusiast. He knew how to take a minus and make a plus out of it. One can have a minus by itself, but one can't have a plus without

189

a minus. And Paul knew how to take a horizontal situation that was negative and cross it with a vertical situation that was positive.

Howard Thurman in his great work, *Deep River and the Negro Spiritual Speaks of Life and Death,* made note of the genius of the Negro slave in the handling of the Jeremiah 8:22 text. He contended:

> The peculiar genius of the Negro slave is revealed here in much of its structural splendor. . . . The setting is the Book of Jeremiah. The prophet has come to a "Dead Sea" place in his life. . . . Jeremiah is actually saying, "There must be a balm in Gilead, it cannot be that there is no balm in Gilead. . . . The slave caught the mood of this spiritual dilemma, and with it did an amazing thing. He straightened out the question mark in Jeremiah's sentence into an exclamation point: "There is a balm in Gilead!" Here is a note of triumph.[4]

Paul said, "This experience is one that has advanced the gospel. I'm not here as a political prisoner. That's not why I'm here. I'm in chains for Christ." I'm here to bear witness for Christ. Paul was saying, "The guards, the palace guards, the praetorian guards are being converted because I'm here." Paul had a knack for taking a prison and turning it into a pulpit. He understood that Christians don't really have jobs; they have ministries. God feeds sparrows and clothes nature. God has His people in the marketplace to minister to people. Paul was saying to the Philippians, "God is using me to fur-

---

4 Howard Thurman, *Deep River and the Negro Spiritual Speaks of Life and Death* (Richmond, IN: Friends University Press, 1975), 55–56.

ther His word right here." Paul turned the prison into a pulpit.

The late great Dr. William Augustus Jones Jr. said, "Daniel was not in the lion's den—the lions were in Daniel's den!" What concerns me about our preachers is that we are turning our pulpits into prisons. We're in bondage. We don't exercise freedom in the pulpit. We have it, but we don't act like we have it. We are being moved because we live in a society where people reject authority. Preachers should not have to beg to be prophetic or ask permission to preach the gospel. No committee should require an evaluation of the sermon before the preacher preaches the sermon. Preachers are not sent to be politically correct or to submit to relativism. God has called the preacher of the gospel to preach a gospel that will either drive or draw people. Paul turned his prison into a pulpit.

In verse 19 he said, "I know that through your prayers and the help given by the Spirit of Jesus Christ, what has happened to me will turn out for my deliverance." Paul declared, "I know that through your prayers and the help of the Spirit . . ."

That word for "help" in Greek is *epichoreagois* from which we get our English word *choreography*. A choreographer is a person who arranges the set and designs the routine of the dance. Paul was saying that God through the Holy Spirit has choreographed my existence. The Spirit of God is our choreographer. I agree with A. W. Tozer. Tozer's fear was that if God took the Holy Spirit out of the world, for twenty-five years the church would keep on doing the same things and wouldn't even know the difference.[5] We have programs, procedures, and mechanics. We have buildings, budgets, and bodies. We have nickels and noses. But we cannot program the Holy Ghost. We need the presence of the Holy Spirit.

The Holy Spirit has really become the stepchild of the Trinity. We don't mind talking about God the Father and God the Son, but in the words of James Forbes, "Many Christians are Holy Spirit-shy."[6] God is not three Gods. God is not three nouns. God is one noun and three adverbial phrases. God the noun is God our Father without skin. God the same noun is the Son, God with skin. And God the same noun is the Holy Spirit, God who gets in our skin.

Paul said, "I know I am going to continue with the help of the Spirit of Jesus Christ, that what has happened to me will turn out for my deliverance." Paul said, "It's going to work out for my deliverance! I'm not sure whether I'm going to stay with you or if I'm going to take a quick exit to be with the Lord, but whatever happens, it's going to work out for my deliverance."

How long can we wait for deliverance? In chapters 1 and 2 of the book of Job, God speaks. In fact God picked Job out to be picked on. Job was minding his business. He didn't know that he was in the book of Job. He didn't even know that his name occupied the title *Job.* God asked Satan, "Have you

---

5 Summarized from writings and sermons of A. W. Tozer; see "How to Be Filled with the Holy Spirit" (Christian Publications pamphlet), "Tozer Speaks to Students" in *Sermons on the Holy Spirit*, ed. Lyle W. Dorsett (Camp Hill, PA: Christian Publishers, 1998); "Tragedy in the Church," in *Sermons on the Spirit and Gifts—Missing in Most Churches* (Camp Hill, PA: Christian Publishers, 1990).
6 James Forbes, *The Holy Spirit and Preaching* (Nashville: Abingdon, 1989), 21.

considered my servant Job?" Job didn't know that God was talking to Satan behind his back! God speaks in chapters 1 and 2. But from chapters 3 through 37, God says nothing. For thirty-five chapters God says absolutely nothing. How long can we wait for God to speak? Can we wait thirty-five chapters?

Some of us are in chapter 30. We've got seven more chapters before we experience a breakthrough in a relationship; seven more chapters before God transforms our church; seven more chapters before God makes clear that God has been moving us from what appeared to be an accident, an incident, or a coincidence to what is unmistakably providence!

God speaks in chapters 38, 39, 40 and 41. In chapter 42, verse 5, we confess like Job, "I had heard of you by the hearing of the ear, but now my eye sees you." God will speak even when God has not spoken for a long time. Paul said, "I know this is going to turn out for my own deliverance."

Finally, verse 27 declares: "Whatever happens . . ." (cp. Phil 1:27 GNB). Paul had said in verse 25, "I know that I will remain, and I will continue with all of you for your progress and joy in the faith." In verse 26 he stated, "That I may share abundantly in your boasting in Christ Jesus when I come to you again." But he's not sure now. "Only conduct yourselves in a manner worthy of the gospel of Christ, so that whether I come and see you or remain absent"—whatever happens—"I will hear of you that you are standing firm in one spirit, with one mind striving together for the faith of the gospel" (v. 27 NASB).

Søren Kierkegaard, the nineteenth-century Danish existentialist philosopher, was right when he contended that life has to be lived forward but can only be understood backwards.[7] There are some things that happen in ministry, in life, in family relationships that we do not immediately perceive as being constructive and beneficial. But if we live long enough and go far enough, we will look back on our lives and can see the permissive will of God promoting God's cause for our good. God will give us strength to live a Romans 8:28 life when we finally get to Rome. Paul wrote Romans 8:28 when he was not in a prison in Rome. He has to have a Romans 8:28 faith now that he is in a Roman prison. "And we know that in all things God works for the good of those who love him, who have been called according to his purpose."

We're looking and living our lives under the very eye and gaze of eternity and from the perspective of God. God is weaving a beautiful tapestry of our life, but we can only see the underneath side of the tapestry. If we could just see what God is doing from the topside, what a difference it would make in the reduction of stress in our life!

Paul lived a "whatever happens" life not because he trusted in fate—*que sera sera,* whatever will be will be—but because he knew that one cannot figure out the "un-figure-out-ableness" of God. One cannot demystify the mystery of God. One cannot unscrew the inscrutability of God. One must trust in the One who works in mysterious ways:

---

7 Søren Kierkegaard, *The Diary of Søren Kierkegaard,* trans. Gerda M. Andersen, ed. Peter P. Rohde (New York: Philosophical Library, 1960), pt. 5, sct. 4, no. 136.

God moves in a mysterious way
His wonders to perform;
He plants His footsteps in the sea
And rides upon the storm.[8]

Paul was not the originator of "living on the edge of whatever happens"; he simply knew the One who modeled it and would enable him to do so: his Lord and Savior, Jesus Christ. In the upper room Jesus and the disciples sang: they went out singing a hymn. He went out to the Mount of Olives where he prayed in Gethsemane. Jesus sang *before* Gethsemane.

Singing must take place before Gethsemane. Gethsemane is that crushing place, the olive press. Three prayers prepared Him for whatever would happen. The first time He prayed, His disciples were asleep. The second time He prayed, He found His disciples asleep again. He prayed, "Father, if it's possible, let this cup pass from me."

Although His disciples were asleep the third time, He prayed, "Not my will but thine be done." It took *three prayers* for him to go from "let this cup pass" to "let Thy will be done." He was arrested outside Gethsemane. On the cross it took *three hours* for Him to go from "My God, why—?" to "Father, into thy. . . ." Twelve o'clock noon looked like twelve o'clock midnight.

It took *three days* for the crucifixion to transition to the resurrection. On Friday He died. On Friday it looked as if the devil had won the battle. On Friday the disciples scattered. Some of them resigned to return to the fishing industry. Friday was a bleak and dark day for the disciples. It was Friday, but

8 William Cowper, "Light Shining Out of Darkness," ca. 1771.

Sunday was coming. On Sunday morning He rose from the dead with all power in His hand—*three days* from the crucifixion to the resurrection.

Jesus stayed on the earth for forty days after the resurrection. At the conclusion of the forty days, He caught a cloud, rode back to glory, and sat down on the right hand of His Father. Today He sits as a high priest making intercession for us. But one day He's going to return and receive believers. Yes!

> All hail the power of Jesus' name!
> Let angels prostrate fall;
> Bring forth the royal diadem, and
> crown Him Lord of all.
> Bring forth the royal diadem, and
> crown Him Lord of all.[9]

If we can just hold out until tomorrow, if we can just keep faith through the night, everything will be all right—regardless of whatever happens!

9 Edward Perronet, "All Hail the Power of Jesus' Name," 1779.

AUTHOR INDEX

SUBJECT INDEX

SCRIPTURE INDEX